Vol. 01

BATTLE CRIES

DECLARATIONS OF **FAITH** FOR **EVERY BATTLE**

Vol. 01

BATTLE CRIES

DECLARATIONS OF FAITH FOR EVERY BATTLE

Theda Vaughan

take heart books

Dedication

To my husband, Ricky, whose steady love has been one of God's greatest gifts to my life. Whose prayers, faith, and unwavering support helped birth every page of this book. **You are a warrior for our family and the Kingdom of God! I thank you with all my heart!**

To my children Dwain, Tristan and Beau and spouses, Keeli and Kaiti and our grandchildren, Travis, Ryker, Dax and Mia. You are each part of the legacy this book carries. I bless your steps, your dreams, your identity, and your future. May you always walk in the fullness of who God created you to be. **You are my greatest earthly gifts and my daily reminder of God's goodness. May your lives always be anchored in Christ Jesus. Use this book to declare your future and connect with God.**

To my church family, Solid Ground Ministries International Inc., thank you for loving, supporting, and encouraging me through every season, thank you for being a community where God's presence is welcomed, His Word is honored, and His people are loved. **Thank you for being warriors, intercessors, and Kingdom builders. Thank you for standing with me as we pursue God's purpose together.**

Battle Cries

19
Section ONE—**For God's Power**

THE ROCK BENEATH MY RISING
NONE CAN WITHSTAND THE HAND OF HEAVEN
I STAND IN AWE IN THE THUNDER OF HIS POWER
LET MY GREY HAIR BLAZE LIKE A BANNER
I SUBMIT TO THE SOVEREIGN HAND
HE WHO NUMBERS THE STARS AND IS BEYOND MEASURE, YET NEAR
BY POWER, BY WISDOM, BY STORM
I KNOW THE WORD. I WALK IN POWER.
HIS POWER CANNOT BE SILENCED
NO EXCUSE. ALL CREATION TESTIFIES.
OVERSHADOWED BY GLORY, EMPOWERED TO BIRTH THE IMPOSSIBLE

***

43
Section TWO—**The Power of Prayers**

I REJOICE—I PRAY—I GIVE THANKS WITHOUT CEASING!
I DO NOT BOW TO ANXIETY—I RISE IN PEACE!
I ASK BOLDLY—HEAVEN HEARS ME!
I WATCH—I PRAY—I GIVE THANKS WITHOUT FAILING!
I CALL—HE LISTENS! I COME—HE RESPONDS!
I ASK IN FAITH—I RECEIVE IN POWER!
I HOPE WITH JOY—I ENDURE WITH STRENGTH—I PRAY WITH FIRE!
I CALL IN TRUTH—HE COMES IN POWER!
I SING IN THE MIDNIGHT—I SHAKE THE DARKNESS!
I CALL—HE ANSWERS! I ASK—HE REVEALS MYSTERIES!

Introduction

by Ricky Vaughan

When Jesus cried out—*It is finished!*—on the cross, He was announcing the greatest wartime victory in history. He was proclaiming His victory over Satan. This signified that our salvation had been won. Jesus' heel had been bruised, but Satan's head had been crushed underneath it. (Gen. 3:15 NIV) What took place over the next three days further established this victory. Revelation 1:18 tells us that He now holds the keys of hell and death. He also disarmed demonic principalities and powers that stood against us and made a bold display and public example of them by triumphing over them through the cross. (Col. 2:15 AMPC) This verse paints a picture of a defeated foe being paraded through the streets by the Victor of a war. "It is finished" was a proclamation by a general who had observed that the victory was here...the enemy is defeated. Jesus used this military battle cry to declare victory over Satan, sin, and death.

Soooo...

Where does that leave us? Are we done? Do we sit back and wait for the rapture?

No! We do not!

Even though victory is ours, there are still battles all around. If you have been walking with God for any amount of time you may have noticed that the enemy is still at work. That's why God tells us that we battle not with flesh and blood, but against principalities, against powers, against the rulers of the darkness of this world, against spiritual wickedness in high places. (Eph. 6:12 KJV)

We are also told that Satan goes about like a roaring lion seeking whom he may devour and for this reason, we are to remain vigilant. (1 Peter 5:8)

Now, as uncomfortable as all this sounds, God has prepared us and equipped us for every situation…including battle with the enemy.

We are told that every good and perfect gift is from above and comes to us from our Heavenly Father. (James 1:17) Have you ever received that less than perfect gift from someone? Perhaps that jelly of the month club or the glow in the dark necktie or even your very own fruitcake.

Well, God is a much better gift giver than that. His gifts all have purpose and great significance. In Ephesians 6, He gives us the whole armor of God. This is not a decorative, passive gift to put on a shelf and look at from time to time. He tells us to "put on" the whole armor so that we can stand against the schemes of the devil. Armor is built for standing…you would be very uncomfortable sitting in armor. (Eph. 6:11 KJV)

In the next few verses God tells us to:
- Stand and gird our waist with truth.
- Put on the breastplate of righteousness.
- Let our feet be fitted with the readiness that comes with the gospel of peace.
- Take up the shield of faith.
- Take and put on the helmet of salvation.
- Take up the sword of the Spirit which is the Word of God.
- Pray in the Spirit with all kinds of prayers and requests.

There's a lot of action there…a further reminder that our salvation and relationship with God is never to be passive, but there are always actions that should correspond with the Word from God. Here, we are told to stand, put on, take up and pray.

This book is about us "taking action" in our relationship with God. It focuses mostly on verse 17, "taking the sword of the Spirit," which is the Word of God.

Words are meant to be spoken!

Our God spoke and created all the heavens and the earth. He spoke what was in His heart into existence. Hebrews 11:3 tells us that the worlds were framed by the Word of God, so that the things which are seen (everything around us and in the entire universe) were not made by things that were visible (but by God's words).

Then in Genesis 1:26 (NKJV) God said, Let us make man in our image, after our likeness: and let them have dominion over the fish of the sea, and over the fowl of the air, and over the cattle, and over all the earth, and over every creeping thing that creeps on the earth.

So, God made us like Him. He made us to speak. He made us to create. He made us to have dominion over all the earth that he had given to man.

All throughout God's Word, He reminds us of the power of our words. Proverbs 18:21 tells us that death and life are in the power of our tongue, and those who love it will eat the fruit thereof. (You will eat death or life.) Your choice! You can speak words of death or words of life. This book is about helping us make wise, Godly choices with our words.

Caution: The following Scripture may be offensive to some! Proceed carefully!

Proverbs 29:11 (MEV) *A fool utters all his mind, but a wise man keeps it in until afterwards.* This is telling us to be careful with our words. They are powerful! They can bring healing or they can cause great damage. Some people are like the novice soldier with his finger locked on a machine gun, spewing uncontrolled damage in every direction. James 3:5-6 further clarifies this: *Likewise, the tongue is a small part of the body, but it makes great boasts. Consider what a great forest is set on fire by a small spark. The tongue also is a fire, a world of evil among the parts of the body. It corrupts the whole body, sets the whole course of one's life on fire, and is itself set on fire by hell.* Your tongue can corrupt every part of your life … or your tongue can bless and bring life to every part of your life.

Our mouth and our words are very important. As we grow in wisdom in our lives, let us make sure we grow in wisdom concerning our words.

When a God (who cannot lie) speaks, then you know that His words are His will. When you know God's will, then you know how you should pray.

This book will be very helpful in your prayer life, making sure your prayers and decrees line up with God's Word and His will.

May you bring the power of God's Word and the blessing of God's promises into every area of your life by allowing these war cries to energize your faith and inspire your prayers.

YOU SHALL ALSO DECIDE AND DECREE A THING, AND IT SHALL BE ESTABLISHED FOR YOU; AND THE LIGHT [OF GOD'S FAVOR] SHALL SHINE UPON YOUR WAYS.

JOB 22:28 (AMPC)

BATTLE CRIES

For
God's Power

The Rock Beneath My Rising

This is a **Battle Cry** that channels its power into a bold anthem–to resonate across generations and stir hearts with reverence and resolve. This is a thunderous declaration of **divine strength, clarity, and unwavering foundation.**

I do not rise by my own strength,
nor stand by fleeting favor.
**I am upheld by the One who was, who is, and
who forever shall be.**

The Lord alone is God.
Not fashioned by hands, nor imagined by minds.
He is the Rock beneath my rising,
the Fortress that girds my soul,
the Architect of every perfect path I walk.

Let the winds howl and the earth tremble—
I shall not be moved.
Let voices rise in accusation—
I shall not be silenced.
Let shadows gather—
I shall not be afraid.

For my God is not a refuge of stone,
but a sanctuary of strength.
He does not merely protect—He perfects.
He does not simply shield—He shapes.

So I declare with unwavering breath
My steps are ordered.
My footing is firm.
My future is forged in the fire of His faithfulness.

There is no other.
There is no equal.
There is no god but the LORD.

For who is God except the Lord? Who but our God is a solid rock? God is my strong fortress, and he makes my way perfect. — 2 Samuel 32:33 (NLT)

None Can Withstand the Hand of Heaven

This is a **Battle Cry** that captures the majesty of Jehoshaphat's words and transforms them into a bold, multi-generational anthem of trust, authority, and unwavering allegiance.

I do not tremble before the nations.
I do not bow to earthly powers.
I stand in the house of the Lord,
where covenant echoes through generations,
and the throne of heaven rules without rival.

You are the God of our fathers—
the Keeper of promises, the Ruler of realms.
You reign above every kingdom,
and command every battle with sovereign might.

In Your hand is power that cannot be broken.
In Your hand is might that cannot be matched.
In Your hand is victory before the war begins.

So I declare
Let every enemy see Your hand and flee.
Let every fear dissolve in Your presence.
Let every heart rise in holy confidence.

For You, O Lord, are enthroned in heaven.
You reign over nations, generations, and destinies.
And none—no force, no foe, no shadow—can withstand You.

And Jehoshaphat stood in the assembly of Judah and Jerusalem, in the house of the LORD before the new court and said, "O LORD God of our fathers, are you not God in heaven? You rule over all the kingdoms of the nations. In your hand are power and might, so that none is able to withstand you." — 2 Chronicles 20:6 (NLT)

I Stand in Awe in the Thunder of His Power

> This is a **Battle Cry** that channels awe into a **declaration of reverence, authority, and spiritual confidence.** It echoes across generations, stirring hearts to stand in the shadow of His thunder. **It is a breathtaking portrait of** divine majesty—cosmic, poetic, and terrifying in its beauty.

I do not fight alone.
I do not speak from dust.
I rise beneath the sky He stretched over nothing,
and walk upon the earth He hung in the void.

He wraps the rain in clouds that do not burst.
He veils the moon in mystery.
He carves the horizon with His breath
and draws the line between day and night.

The foundations of heaven tremble at His rebuke.
The sea bows to His voice.
The serpent is pierced by His hand.
The monster is crushed beneath His wisdom.

So I declare—
I am not afraid of chaos—He calms it.
I am not shaken by darkness—He commands it.
I am not overwhelmed by mystery—He authored it.

His Spirit adorns the heavens with beauty.
His power thunders beyond comprehension.
And I—child of covenant, heir of promise—
stand in the echo of His whisper
and move in the wake of His roar.

Let every enemy know:
I am aligned with the One who commands the cosmos.
I am upheld by the One who rebukes the deep.
I am empowered by the whisper that shakes worlds.

**This is not the fullness of His strength—
this is only the beginning.
And even that is enough to make the heavens tremble.**

God stretches the northern sky over empty space and hangs the earth on nothing. He wraps the rain in his thick clouds, and the clouds don't burst with the weight. He covers the face of the moon, shrouding it with his clouds. He created the horizon when he separated the waters: he set the boundary between day and night. The foundations of heaven tremble; they shudder at his rebuke. By his power the sea grew calm. By his skill he crushed the great sea monster. His Spirit made the heavens beautiful, and his power pierced the gliding serpent. These are just the beginning of all that he does, merely a whisper of his power. Who, then, can comprehend the thunder of his power? —Job 26:7-14 (NLT)

Let My Grey Hair Blaze Like a Banner

This is a **Battle Cry** that honors the wisdom of age, the authority of experience, and the sacred call to proclaim **God's power** to those who follow. It carries the fire of testimony, and the urgency of generational transfer.

I do not fade—I flame.
Though my hair is silver, my spirit is steel.
Though my steps may slow, my voice still thunders with truth.

I have seen the miracles.
I have walked through fire and flood.
I have tasted the faithfulness of God in every season.

So I declare
Do not silence me—send me.
Do not retire me—refire me.
Do not let me vanish—let me be visible.

I will proclaim His power to the children yet unborn.
I will speak of His wonders to those who have never seen.
I will pass the torch, not drop it.

Let this generation know:
The God of my youth is the God of their future.
The miracles of my past are the promises of their tomorrow.
The legacy I carry is the light they will walk by.

I may be old and grey,
but I am crowned with testimony,
clothed in wisdom,
and commissioned to roar.

**Let my life be a living scroll.
Let my words be a war cry.
Let my witness awaken the next wave of warriors.**

Now that I am old and grey, do not abandon me, O God. Let me proclaim your power to this new generation, your mighty miracles to all who come after me. — Psalm 71:18 (NLT)

I Submit to the Sovereign Hand

This is a **Battle Cry** that honors God's supreme authority while calling His people to walk in **wisdom, humility, and spiritual discernment** under His leadership.

I do not bow to man—I bow to the One who enthrones kings.
I do not fear rulers—I fear the Lord who rules over all.
Every crown, every court, every command is beneath His throne.

He appoints. He permits. He prevails.
No authority stands apart from His decree.
No leader rises without His knowing.
No law is beyond His reach.

So I declare ⸺
I walk in honor, not rebellion.
I submit in strength, not silence.
I discern with wisdom, not fear.

For my allegiance is first to the Kingdom,
but I walk faithfully in the land He has placed me.
I will not resist what He has ordained.
I will not forget that even earthly power is held in
heavenly hands.

Let every authority know:
I am governed by grace.
I am led by truth.

I am submitted to the Sovereign Hand.

And when the time comes to speak,
I will speak with boldness.
When the time comes to stand,
I will stand in righteousness.
For I serve the King above all kings,
and His justice will not sleep.

Everyone must submit to governing authorities. For all authority comes from God, and those in positions of authority have been placed there by God.
— Romans 13:1 (NLT)

He Who Numbers the Stars and is Beyond Measure, Yet Near

This is a **Battle Cry** that captures the majesty of the One who names stars and knows hearts. It is a declaration of **God's authority, intimate care, and immeasurable wisdom.**

I rise under skies He stretched with His hand.
I walk beneath constellations He called by name.
Not one star escapes His gaze—
Not one soul is forgotten in His heart.

He is the Architect of galaxies,
the Whisperer of names,
the Keeper of mysteries too vast for measure.

So I declare
I am not lost in the crowd.
I am not overlooked in the chaos.
I am known. I am named. I am chosen.

His power is not distant—it is near.
His wisdom is not unreachable—it is guiding me now.
His greatness does not diminish His tenderness.

I will not fear the unknown,
for I am held by the One who knows all.
I will not shrink beneath the stars,
for I am called by the same voice that named them.

Let every doubt be silenced.
Let every lie be scattered like stardust.
I belong to the Infinite—
and He has written my name among the heavens.

He determines the number of the stars; he gives to all of them their names. Great is our Lord, and abundant in power; his understanding is beyond measure.
— Psalm 147:4-5 (NLT)

By Power, By Wisdom, By Storm

This is a **Battle Cry** that the power of God's voice is the sustaining wisdom that holds creation together. It is an song of divine craftsmanship and authority.

I do not stand on random soil—
I stand on ground shaped by His hand.
I do not breathe borrowed air—
I inhale the breath of divine wisdom.

The skies above me are not empty.
They are stretched by understanding,
woven with purpose,
and alive with the voice of the Almighty.

So I declare
When thunder rolls, I do not tremble.
When lightning strikes, I do not scatter.
For the storm is not chaos—it is command.
The rain is not wrath—it is release.
The wind is not wild—it is sent.

He speaks, and the heavens respond.
He commands, and creation obeys.
He sustains, and I endure.

Let every cloud remind me:
I am preserved by wisdom.

Let every roar remind me:
I am protected by power.
Let every gust remind me:
I am propelled by purpose.

I walk in the wake of His voice.
I rise in the rhythm of His reign.
I am not shaken—I am summoned.
By power, by wisdom, by storm—I go forth.

But God made the earth by his power, and he preserves it by his wisdom. With his own understanding, he stretched out the heavens. When he speaks in the thunder, the heavens roar with rain. He causes the clouds to rise over the earth. He sends the lightning with the rain and releases the wind from his storehouses. — Jeremiah 10:12-13 (NLT)

I Know the Word. I Walk in Power.

This is a **Battle Cry** that **confronts spiritual apathy and summons bold, scriptural authority**. It is a piercing call to spiritual awareness. A reminder that ignorance of the Word and the power behind it leads to error.

I will not be found lacking.
I will not be led astray.
I know the Word—and the Word knows me.
I walk in power—not theory, not form, but fire.

I declare
**I am not deceived by clever arguments.
I am not silenced by worldly wisdom.
I am rooted in truth,
and ignited by the Spirit.**

The Scriptures are my sword.
The power of God is my shield.
I do not serve a distant deity—I serve a living King.
His Word is alive in me.
His power flows through me.

Let every lie be exposed.
Let every confusion be cleared.
Let every heart awaken to the voice of truth.

**I rise with revelation.
I stand in demonstration.**

I speak with authority.
I move with heaven's force.

I will not be mistaken.
I know the Scriptures.
I know the power of God.
And I will not be silent.

Jesus replied, "Your mistake is that you don't know the Scriptures, and you don't know the power of God."
— Matthew 22:29 (NLT)

His Power Cannot Be Silenced

This is a **Battle Cry** that captures the wildfire spread of His healing, His voice, and His undeniable presence. It pulses with unstoppable momentum—Jesus' power couldn't be contained, and the hunger of the people broke through every barrier.

I serve the One whose power defies containment.
No command, no wall, no silence can hold back His glory.
When He moves, the earth responds.
When He speaks, the broken rise.

So I declare
His name will not be hidden.
His works will not be hushed.
His healing will not be halted.

Let the crowds come.
Let the desperate press in.
Let the wounded hear His voice.
Let the sick touch His robe.

I carry the report.
I echo the roar.
I spread the fire.

For His power is not a secret—
It is a summons.
His presence is not a whisper—
It is a wave.

I will not be quiet.
I will not be still.
I will not be ashamed.

The world will know:
He heals.
He speaks.
He saves.
And His power cannot be silenced.

But despite Jesus' instructions, the report of his power spread even faster, and vast crowds came to hear him preach and to be healed of their diseases. — Luke 5:15 (NLT)

No Excuse. All Creation Testifies.

This is a **Battle Cry** that turns truth into a bold, generational anthem. This is a declaration that creation itself is a witness–a living scroll that proclaims God's eternal power and divine nature.

I do not walk blind—I walk beneath a sky that shouts.
I do not question His existence—creation confirms it
with every breath.
The mountains echo His strength.
The oceans reflect His depth.
The stars blaze with His glory.

So I declare
I will not be silent when the trees are clapping.
I will not be still when the rivers are running with praise.
I will not doubt when the heavens are preaching.

His power is eternal.
His nature is divine.
And the earth is drenched in His fingerprints.

Let every sunrise remind me: **He is faithful.**
Let every storm remind me: **He is mighty.**
Let every creature remind me: **He is Creator.**

I will not make excuses.
I will not plead ignorance.
I will not pretend the evidence is hidden.

I know Him—because the world knows Him.
I see Him—because the sky sees Him.
I worship Him—because all creation does.

No excuse. No retreat.
I rise with the testimony of the earth.
I roar with the witness of the heavens.
I stand with the voice of creation—
And I declare: HE IS GOD.

For ever since the world was created, people have seen the earth and sky. Through everything God made, they can clearly see his invisible qualities – his eternal power, and divine nature. So, they have no excuse for not knowing God.
—Romans 1:20 (NLT)

BATTLE CRY

Overshadowed by Glory, Empowered to Birth the Impossible

This is a **Battle Cry** that speaks of the moment heaven touched earth, and the impossible bowed to the authority of the Most High. It captures the awe of that encounter and transforms it into a declaration of **God's unstoppable, overshadowing power.**

I do not walk in ordinary strength.
I am overshadowed by glory.
I am filled by the Spirit.
I am chosen to carry what the world cannot conceive.

The power of the Most High is not distant—it descends.
It does not merely visit—it inhabits.
It does not whisper—it overshadows.

So I declare
Let the impossible be conceived.
Let the holy be born through me.
Let the power of God rewrite my story.

I am not barren—I am blessed.
I am not forgotten—I am favored.
I am not weak—I am overshadowed.

The same Spirit that hovered over Mary hovers over me.
The same power that formed the Son of God now forms purpose in me.

The same overshadowing presence now commissions me
to carry heaven to earth.

Let every fear fall silent.
Let every doubt dissolve.
Let every promise rise.

For I am overshadowed by the Most High,
and what I carry will be holy,
and what I birth will shake nations.

The angel replied, "The Holy Spirit will come upon you, and
the power of the Most High will overshadow you. So, the
baby to be born will be holy, and he will be called the Son of
God." — Luke 1:35 (NLT)

BATTLE CRIES

For
The Power of Prayers

BATTLE CRY

I Rejoice—I Pray—I Give Thanks Without Ceasing!

This is the **Battle Cry** of a warrior whose strength flows from joy, whose power is sustained by prayer, and whose victory is sealed in gratitude. It's a declaration that no circumstance can silence the song, stop the prayer, or steal the praise.

I do not wait for ease—*I rejoice in the storm*!
I do not pause in battle—*I pray without ceasing!*
I do not give thanks for comfort—*I give thanks in every circumstance!*

Joy is my resistance.
Prayer is my power.
Gratitude is my ground—*and this is God's will for me!*

I declare
I will not be ruled by emotion—I am anchored in rejoicing!
I will not be drained by struggle—I am fueled by prayer!
I will not be silenced by hardship—I am loud with thanksgiving!

My joy is not fragile—it's forged in fire.
My prayers are not weak—they are weapons of war.
My thanks is not passive—it's a proclamation of victory!

So I cry out with fierce joy and holy rhythm:
I rejoice—I pray—I give thanks without ceasing!

I do not waver—I worship!
I do not retreat—I release praise!

Let trials come—I answer with triumph.
Let weariness whisper—I respond with worship.
Let chaos rise—I roar: *This is God's will for me in Christ Jesus!*

This is my battle cry
I do not just endure—I exalt!
I do not just survive—I saturate the air with prayer!
I do not just hope—I harness heaven with thanksgiving!
*I am a warrior of rhythm—rejoicing, praying, and praising
without end!*

Rejoice always, pray continually, give thanks in all circumstances; for this is God's will for you in Christ Jesus.
—1 Thessalonians 5:16-18 (NIV)

I Do Not Bow to Anxiety—I Rise in Peace!

This is the **Battle Cry** of a warrior who refuses to be ruled by fear, who fights with prayer, and who is guarded by supernatural peace. It's a declaration that anxiety has no throne, and peace is the armor of the faithful.

I do not tremble—*I petition with power!*
I do not spiral—*I pray with precision!*
I do not panic—*I give thanks with boldness!*

Anxiety is not my master—*prayer is my weapon!*
Fear is not my fortress—*peace is my shield!*
Confusion is not my companion—*Christ guards my mind!*

I declare

I will not be anxious—I am anchored in intercession!
I will not be overwhelmed—I am overshadowed by peace!
I will not be silenced—I speak my needs with
thanksgiving!

My heart is not exposed—*it is guarded by glory!*
My mind is not vulnerable—*it is fortified by Christ!*
My soul is not scattered—*it is centered in divine calm!*

So I cry out with fierce faith and holy stillness:
I do not bow to anxiety—I rise in peace!
I do not fear the unknown—I present it to God!
I do not carry the weight—I cast it in prayer!

Let pressure press—I respond with petition.
Let worry whisper—I answer with worship.
Let chaos stir—I stand in the stillness of God.

This is my battle cry—
I do not just cope—I conquer through communion!
I do not just endure—I exchange fear for peace!
I do not just survive—I stand guarded by the Prince of Peace!
I am a warrior of stillness—praying, thanking, and trusting
without fear!

Do not be anxious about anything, but in every situation, by prayer and petition, with thanksgiving, present your requests to God. And the peace of God, which transcends all understanding, will guard your hearts and your minds in Christ Jesus. —Philippians 4:6-7 (NIV)

I Ask Boldly—Heaven Hears Me!

This is the **Battle Cry** of a warrior who knows their voice shakes heaven, whose confidence is rooted in divine alignment, and whose prayers are not whispers but war cries. It's a declaration that God is not distant, He is attentive, responsive, and ready to move.

I do not beg—*I boldly approach!*
I do not doubt—*I declare with confidence!*
I do not speak into silence—*I am heard by the throne of God!*

My confidence is not in outcome—*it's in access!*
My strength is not in volume—*it's in alignment!*
My power is not in persuasion—*it's in His will!*

I declare
I am not timid—I am *authorized!*
I am not ignored—I am *heard!*
I am not uncertain—I am *anchored in His will!*

Heaven is not deaf—*it is attentive to my cry!*
God is not distant—*He is near to my voice!*
My prayers are not lost—*they are received with divine precision!*

So I cry out with fierce faith and holy fire:
I ask boldly—Heaven hears me!
I do not shrink—I stand in confidence!
I do not guess—I align with His will and speak with authority!

Let doubt rise—I respond with confidence.
Let silence threaten—I roar with truth.
Let fear whisper—I answer with faith.

This is my battle cry—
I do not just speak—*I summon heaven!*
I do not just hope—*I ask according to His will!*
I do not just wish—*I wield the weapon of prayer!*
I am a warrior of confidence—heard, known, and backed
by the will of God!

This is the confidence we have in approaching God: that if
we ask anything according to his will, he hears us.
—1 John 5:14 (NIV)

I Watch—I Pray—I Give Thanks Without Failing!

This is the Battle Cry of a vigilant warrior whose devotion is fierce, whose eyes are open, and whose heart overflows with gratitude. It's a declaration that prayer is not passive, it's a posture of power, a stance of readiness, and a rhythm of thanksgiving.

I do not drift—*I devote myself to prayer!*
I do not sleep through battle—*I stay watchful!*
I do not grumble—*I give thanks with fire!*

Prayer is my discipline—*not my last resort!*
Watchfulness is my posture—*not my weakness!*
Thanksgiving is my rhythm—*not my reaction!*

I declare
I am not distracted—*I am devoted!*
I am not blind—*I am awake and alert!*
I am not bitter—*I am grateful in every breath!*

My prayers are not empty—*they are charged with purpose!*
My eyes are not closed—*they are fixed on the move of God!*
My heart is not hardened—*it is softened by thanksgiving!*

So I cry out with fierce focus and holy rhythm:
I watch—I pray—I give thanks without failing!
I do not slumber—I stand in devotion!
I do not forget—I remain faithful in prayer!

Let distraction come—I answer with devotion.
Let weariness whisper—I respond with watchfulness.
Let heaviness press—I rise with thanksgiving.

This is my battle cry
I do not just speak—*I stay in communion!*
I do not just react—*I remain rooted in prayer!*
I do not just endure—*I overflow with thanks!*
I am a warrior of devotion—watchful, prayerful, and
grateful in every season!

Devote yourselves to prayer, being watchful and thankful.
—Colossians 4:2 (NIV)

BATTLE CRY 

I Call—He Listens! I Come—He Responds!

This is the **Battle Cry** of a warrior who knows that heaven bends low when they speak, that prayer is not a ritual but a divine encounter, and that God is not distant, He is listening, leaning in, and ready to move.

I do not whisper into the void—I call on the Living God!
I do not wander—I come with purpose and fire!
I do not speak in vain—He listens when I pray!

My voice is not lost—*it is heard in heaven!*
My prayers are not ignored—*they are received by the King!*
My approach is not denied—*it is welcomed by the Father!*

I declare

I am not forgotten—*I am heard!*
I am not rejected—*I am received!*
I am not alone—*I am met by the One who listens!*

I call with confidence—*He answers with compassion!*
I come with boldness—*He responds with presence!*
I pray with fire—*He listens with love!*

So I cry out with fierce faith and holy expectation:
I call—He listens! I come—He responds!
I do not hesitate—I approach with fire!
I do not doubt—I am heard by the God who moves!

Let silence threaten—I answer with prayer.
Let distance deceive—I respond with pursuit.
Let fear whisper—I roar with truth: *"He listens to me!"*

This is my battle cry
I do not just speak—*I ignite divine dialogue!*
I do not just hope—*I engage the heart of God!*
I do not just ask—*I am heard by the One who reigns!*
I am a warrior of communion—calling, coming, and
praying with fire, knowing my God listens!

Then you will call on me and come and pray to me, and I will listen to you. —Jeremiah 29:12 (NIV)

I Ask in Faith—I Receive in Power!

This is the **Battle Cry** of a warrior who prays with bold belief, who sees with spiritual eyes, and who stands in the certainty of heaven's promise. It's a declaration that faith is not fragile, it's fierce, and that what is asked in alignment with God is already secured in the spirit.

I do not beg—*I believe!*
I do not wish—*I war with faith!*
I do not wait in fear—*I receive with fire!*

My prayers are not empty—*they are backed by belief!*
My faith is not passive—*it is aggressive in trust!*
My asking is not timid—*it is charged with divine confidence!*

I declare
I ask with boldness—*and I receive with certainty!*
I believe before I see—*and I walk as one who already holds the promise!*
I do not doubt—*I stand in the reality of answered prayer!*

Heaven does not delay—*it responds to faith!*
My words are not wasted—*they are seeds of victory!*
My heart is not hesitant—*it is anchored in divine assurance!*

So I cry out with fierce trust and holy boldness:

I ask in faith—I receive in power!
I do not flinch—I believe and possess!
I do not stagger—I stand in the promise!

Let delay come—I respond with belief.
Let doubt whisper—I roar with trust.
Let impossibility rise—I answer with faith.

This is my battle cry—
I do not just pray—*I possess the promise!*
I do not just hope—*I hold what I've asked for in faith!*
I do not just speak—*I stand in supernatural certainty!*
I am a warrior of belief—asking, receiving, and walking
in the fullness of what is mine!

Therefore, I tell you, whatever you ask for in prayer, believe
that you have received it, and it will be yours.
—Mark 11:24 (NIV)

I Hope with Joy—I Endure with Strength—I Pray with Fire!

> This is the **Battle Cry** of a warrior who refuses to be shaken by delay, who stands firm in suffering, and who stays lit with relentless prayer. It's a declaration that joy is not circumstantial, patience is not weakness, and prayer is not optional. It's the rhythm of the resilient.

I do not despair—*I hope with joy!*
I do not break—*I endure with patience!*
I do not fade—*I pray with fire!*

My joy is not fragile—*it is fueled by hope!*
My patience is not passive—*it is powered by purpose!*
My prayer is not routine—*it is relentless warfare!*

I declare
I rejoice in what's coming—*even when I don't see it yet!*
I endure what's pressing—*because I know who holds me!*
I pray without quitting—*because heaven moves when I speak!*

Affliction does not define me—*faithfulness does!*
Delay does not defeat me—*hope sustains me!*
Silence does not stop me—*prayer ignites me!*

So I cry out with fierce joy and holy resolve:
I hope with joy—I endure with strength—I pray with fire!
I do not quit—I rise!
I do not crumble—I conquer!

Let affliction press—I respond with patience.
Let waiting stretch—I answer with joy.
Let weariness whisper—I roar with prayer.

This is my battle cry—
I do not just survive—*I shine with hope!*
I do not just endure—*I stand with purpose!*
I do not just speak—*I storm heaven with prayer!*
I am a warrior of rhythm—joyful, patient, and faithful in
every season!

Be joyful in hope, patient in affliction, faithful in prayer.
-—Romans 12:12 (NIV)

BATTLE CRY

I Call in Truth—He Comes in Power!

This is the **Battle Cry** of a warrior who knows that truth draws God close, that honesty is holy, and that calling on the Lord is not a ritual–it's a summons for divine presence. It's a declaration that God is not far off, He is near, attentive, and ready to respond to the voice of the sincere.

I do not call in pretense—*I call in truth!*
I do not speak to the air—*I summon the nearness of God!*
I do not hide—*I cry out with raw faith and real fire!*

My truth is not weakness—*it is a weapon of intimacy!*
My cry is not ignored—*it is answered with presence!*
My voice is not lost—*it is heard by the One who draws near!*

I declare
I call with honesty—*and He comes with power!*
I speak with sincerity—*and He surrounds me with strength!*
I cry out in truth—*and He responds with nearness!*

I am not abandoned—*I am met by the Lord!*
I am not overlooked—*I am embraced by His presence!*
I am not alone—*I am surrounded by the nearness of God!*

So I cry out with fierce truth and holy expectation:
I call in truth—He comes in power!
I do not pretend—I pursue!
I do not perform—I proclaim!

Let distance threaten—I respond with truth.
Let silence linger—I answer with sincerity.
Let fear whisper—I roar with reality: *"The Lord is near to me!"*

This is my battle cry—
I do not just speak—*I summon the nearness of heaven!*
I do not just hope—*I call with truth and stand in presence!*
I do not just cry—*I am heard, known, and met by the Lord!*
I am a warrior of truth—calling, believing, and walking with the God who draws near!

The Lord is near to all who call on him, to all who call on him in truth. —Psalm 145:18 (NIV)

I Sing in the Midnight—I Shake the Darkness!

> This is the **Battle Cry** of a warrior who worships in chains, who prays in the dark, and whose praise becomes a weapon that breaks through prison walls. It's a declaration that midnight is not the end, it's the moment heaven invades, and that praise is powerful enough to echo through captivity and awaken freedom.

I do not wait for daylight—*I worship in the midnight!*
I do not wait for freedom—*I pray in the prison!*
I do not wait for comfort—*I sing in the storm!*

My praise is not quiet—*it is a battle cry in the dark!*
My prayer is not weak—*it is a force that shakes foundations!*
My voice is not silenced—*it is a sound that awakens others!*

I declare ————
I sing when others sleep—*and chains begin to rattle!*
I pray when others despair—*and heaven begins to move!*
I worship when walls surround me—*and breakthrough begins to roar!*

Midnight does not mute me—*it magnifies my praise!*
Captivity does not crush me—*it calls forth my cry!*
Darkness does not define me—*it is the stage for my song!*

So I cry out with fierce worship and holy defiance:
I sing in the midnight—I shake the darkness!

I do not wait—I war with praise!
I do not break—I break through!

Let chains tighten—I respond with hymns.
Let silence press—I answer with song.
Let despair whisper—I roar with prayer.

This is my battle cry—
I do not just endure—*I ignite the atmosphere!*
I do not just survive—*I sing until walls fall!*
I do not just hope—*I worship until heaven invades!*
I am a warrior of midnight—praying, praising, and
shaking the prison with my voice!

About midnight Paul and Silas were praying and singing hymns to God, and the other prisoners were listening to them. —Acts 16:25 (NIV)

I Call—He Answers! I Ask—He Reveals Mysteries!

This is the **Battle Cry** of a warrior who knows that heaven is not silent, that divine secrets are unlocked through prayer, and that revelation is the reward of the bold. It's a declaration that calling on God is not just communication, it's invitation into the unknown, into greatness, into glory.

I do not speak to the wind—*I call to the Almighty!*
I do not settle for surface—*I ask for the unsearchable!*
I do not walk blind—*I receive divine insight!*

My voice is not ignored—*it is answered with revelation!*
My questions are not wasted—*they are keys to hidden things!*
My pursuit is not empty—*it is met with mysteries revealed!*

I declare
I call with confidence—*and heaven responds!*
I ask with boldness—*and secrets unfold!*
I seek with fire—*and greatness is revealed!*

I am not left in the dark—*I am lit by divine wisdom!*
I am not denied access—*I am invited into the depths of God!*
I am not forgotten—*I am spoken to by the One who knows all things!*

So I cry out with fierce hunger and holy expectation:
I call—He answers! I ask—He reveals!

I do not wander—I walk in revelation!
I do not guess—I receive what eyes have not seen!

Let mystery surround—I respond with pursuit.
Let confusion rise—I answer with communion.
Let silence threaten—I roar with trust: *"He will tell me great and unsearchable things!"*

This is my battle cry—
I do not just speak—*I unlock heaven's secrets!*
I do not just pray—*I receive what cannot be known by man!*
I do not just hope—*I walk in the wisdom of the Most High!*
I am a warrior of revelation—calling, receiving, and moving in the mysteries of God!

Call to me and I will answer you and tell you great and unsearchable things you do not know.
—Jeremiah 33:3 (NIV)

BATTLE CRIES

For
The Power of Your Words

BATTLE CRY

My Voice is Holy—My Heart is Aligned!

I do not speak carelessly—*my words are weapons of worship!*
I do not think aimlessly—*my heart meditates on truth!*
I do not seek approval from man—*I live to please the One who redeemed me! HEAR ME, DARKNESS:*

My mouth will not echo your lies—it declares the Word of God!
My heart will not dwell in fear—it meditates on the Rock of salvation!
My life will not drift—I am anchored in the Redeemer's gaze!

Every word I speak is a flame—*let it burn with righteousness!*
Every thought I hold is a seed—*let it grow in holiness!*
Every breath I take is a vow—*let it rise as a pleasing offering!*

My mouth is not a tool of destruction—*it is a trumpet of truth!*
My heart is not a battlefield of confusion—*it is a sanctuary of divine meditation!*
My Redeemer is not distant—*He is near, watching, strengthening, delighting in me!*

I do not fight with noise—*I fight with words forged in heaven!*
I do not meditate on weakness—*I meditate on the Rock who cannot be moved!*
I do not seek fleeting praise—*I seek eternal approval from the One who saved me! So I cry out with holy fire:*

Let my words be pure—my mouth is a vessel of glory!
Let my heart be focused—my thoughts are arrows of truth!
Let my life be pleasing—my Rock is watching, my Redeemer is near!

Let every careless word fall silent.
Let every wandering thought be brought into alignment.
Let every warrior speak and think with purpose, power, and purity.

This is my battle cry ⊢———— *My mouth speaks life, my heart breathes truth!*
I do not war with empty words—I war with holy declarations.
I do not drift in thought—I meditate with fire.
I do not stand alone—I stand on the Rock, redeemed and ready!

Let the words of my mouth and the meditation of my heart be acceptable in Your sight, O Lord, my rock and my Redeemer. — Psalm 19:14 (NASB)

My Tongue is a Sword of Truth—Lies Have No Place Here!

This is a **Battle Cry** that is a covenantal declaration, perfect for legacy, ministry, and spiritual authority. It is a fierce call to integrity. **A sword against deception and a shield for truth.**

I do not speak to destroy—*I speak to deliver!*
I do not twist truth—*I declare it boldly!*
I do not entertain deception—my *lips are sealed with righteousness! Hear me, falsehood:*

You will not pass through my mouth—truth is my only language!
You will not stain my lips—my words are washed in fire!
You will not shape my speech—I speak as one called to holiness!

Evil speech is a snare—*I cut it loose with truth!*
Lies are poison—*I purge them with purity!*
My tongue is not a weapon of darkness—*it is a trumpet of light!*

My lips are not for flattery—*they are for fierce declarations of justice!*
My voice is not for manipulation—*it is for magnifying the King!*
My words are not empty—*they are filled with power, purpose, and purity!*

I do not whisper deceit—*I shout truth with boldness!*
I do not curse—*I bless with fire and conviction!*
I do not speak evil—*I speak life, and I speak it loud!*

So I cry out with holy defiance:
My tongue will not serve evil—it serves the living God!
My lips will not lie—they proclaim truth without fear!
My voice will not falter—it is forged in righteousness!

Let every false word fall silent. Let every deceptive tongue
be stilled.
Let every warrior rise with lips purified and tongues
sharpened by truth.

This is my battle cry — *I do not speak to please
darkness, I speak to pierce it!*
I do not lie—I liberate.
I do not curse—I consecrate.
I do not whisper evil—I roar with truth!

Then keep your tongue from speaking evil and your lips from
telling lies! — Psalm 34:13 (NLT)

Guard My Mouth, Lord—Let No Darkness Pass These Gates

This is a **Battle Cry** that turns into a bold declaration of spiritual discipline, legacy, and authority. It is a cry for holy restraint, a call to consecrate the mouth as a gate of righteousness and protection.

I do not speak without purpose—
my words are watched by heaven!
I do not open my lips to destruction—*they are gates of glory!*
I do not trust my tongue alone—*I call on the Lord to guard every word!*

Hear me, corruption:
You will not slip past my lips—
God stands watch at the gate!
You will not twist my tongue—truth is my language, and holiness my tone!
You will not use my voice—I surrender it to the King of rightcousness!

My mouth is not a weapon of chaos—
it is a sanctuary of truth!
My lips are not doors to destruction—*they are sealed by divine command!*
My speech is not careless—*it is consecrated, guarded, and guided!*

The Lord is my watchman—*I do not speak without His light!*

The door of my lips is fortified—*I do not open it to evil!*
My words are not mine alone
—they are echoes of heaven's heart!

I do not fight with volume—*I fight with virtue!*
I do not speak to wound—*I speak to heal, to build, to bless!*
I do not let my tongue wander—*I bind it to the will of God!*

So I cry out with fierce surrender:
Lord, set Your guard—I will not speak without Your command!
Lord, watch my lips—let no darkness pass through!
Lord, consecrate my voice—make it a vessel of Your glory!

Let every careless word be silenced.
Let every guarded mouth speak with power.
Let every warrior rise with lips sealed by holiness and tongues trained for truth.

This is my battle cry
My mouth is not mine, it is His!
I do not speak to stir strife—I speak to summon light.
I do not open my lips to evil—I open them to eternity.
I do not trust my tongue—I trust the One who guards it!

Set a guard over my mouth, Lord; keep watch over the door of my lips. — Psalm 141:3 (NIV)

I Speak with Fire or Not at All— Silence is My Strength

This **Battle Cry** is a bold declaration of spiritual discipline, protection, and covenant speech. This cry is a sharp, sobering call to restraint, a reminder that **silence can be a weapon of wisdom**.

I do not speak to be heard—*I speak to bring heaven!*
I do not fill the air with noise—*I fill it with purpose or stay silent!*
I do not let words run wild—*I reign them in with wisdom and fire!*

Hear me, idle chatter:
You will not lead me to sin—
I shut the door and seal it with sense!
You will not waste my breath—I speak only what builds, blesses, or breaks chains!
You will not rule my tongue—I silence you with strength and self-control!

My silence is not weakness—*it is a weapon of restraint!*
My quiet is not fear—*it is fierce discipline!*
My words are not many—*they are measured, mighty, and meaningful!*

I do not speak to impress—*I speak to impact!*
I do not talk to fill space—*I let silence speak louder than sin!*
I do not babble—*I build with every syllable or say nothing at all!*

I do not fight with noise—*I fight with precision!*
I do not war with empty words—*I war with silence
sharpened by wisdom!*
I do not let my mouth wander—*I bind it to truth and
discipline!*

So I cry out with quiet fire:
**I will not sin with speech—I will speak with strength or
stay silent!**
I will not be reckless—I will be refined!
I will not be loud—I will be lethal with few words!

Let every idle word fall to the ground.
Let every warrior learn the power of silence.
Let every tongue be trained—not to talk, but to triumph.

This is my battle cry ———— *I do not speak to sin, I
speak to strike!*
I do not chatter—I choose clarity.
I do not ramble—I roar with restraint.
I do not fill the air—I fill it with fire or keep it sacred!

Too much talk leads to sin. Be sensible and keep your mouth
shut. — Proverbs 10:19 (NLT)

My Mouth Speaks Wisdom— Deception Will Be Cut Down!

> This is a **Battle Cry** that is a bold declaration of spiritual discernment and covenant speech. It is a fierce contrast between divine wisdom and destructive deceit. **A call to speak with authority, truth, and legacy.**

I do not speak to deceive—*I speak to deliver!*
I do not twist truth—*I release wisdom with every word!*
I do not fear false tongues—*I stand with the sword of discernment in my mouth!*

Hear me, deception:
You will not pass through my lips—*they are consecrated for counsel!*
You will not poison the air—*my voice is a weapon of clarity!*
You will not endure—*your tongue will be cut off by the justice of God!*

My words are not empty—*they are arrows of truth!*
My advice is not casual—*it is crafted in the fire of righteousness!*
My speech is not self-serving—*it is Spirit-led and battle-tested!*

I do not speak to flatter—*I speak to free!*
I do not echo lies—*I declare wisdom that pierces darkness!*
I do not tolerate deceit—*I cut it down with the blade of godly counsel!*

I am not just a voice—*I am a vessel of divine strategy!*
I am not just a speaker—*I am a steward of truth!*
I am not just heard—*I am heaven-backed and hell-shaking!*

So I cry out with righteous fire:
My mouth gives wisdom—because I walk with the Wise
One!
My tongue will not deceive—it will divide truth from lies!
I do not speak to survive—I speak to strike down
deception!

Let every false tongue be silenced.
Let every godly voice rise with clarity.
Let every warrior speak with wisdom that wounds the
enemy and heals the broken.

This is my battle cry ⸺ *I do not speak to
impress, I speak to impact!*
I do not tolerate lies—I tear them down.
I do not whisper deceit—I roar with truth.
I do not speak for myself—I speak for the Kingdom!

The mouth of the godly person gives wise advice, but the
tongue that deceives will be cut off. — Proverbs 10:31 (NKJV)

My Words Are Weapons of Wisdom!

> This is a **Battle Cry** that makes a bold, declaration of impact, authority, and generational blessing. It is **a reminder that words—when rooted in wisdom—don't just echo, they build.**

I do not speak to be heard—*I speak to bring heaven's reward!*
I do not echo noise—*I release wisdom that multiplies strength!*
I do not waste breath—*I forge every word like a blade of blessing!*

Let the foolish chatter fall away—*my voice is sharpened by truth!*
Let empty talk be silenced—*my speech is soaked in divine strategy!*
Let confusion be scattered—*my words bring clarity, courage, and conquest!*

Every wise word I speak is a seed of victory.
Every phrase forged in truth is a path to breakthrough.
Every sentence shaped by the Spirit is a storm against stagnation.

I speak not to flatter—*I speak to fortify!*
I speak not to entertain—*I speak to empower!*
I speak not to impress—*I speak to ignite transformation!*

My mouth is a fountain of favor.
My tongue is a tool of triumph.
My voice is a vessel of vision.

So I cry out with fire in my bones:
My words are wise—and they bring healing, strength, and strategy!
My speech is seasoned—*and it multiplies miracles!*
My declarations are divine—*and they unlock destiny!*

Let every wise word be a weapon.
Let every benefit be a banner of victory.
Let every voice aligned with truth rise like thunder.

This is my battle cry *I speak with purpose, I speak with power, I speak with wisdom that wins!*
I do not speak to survive—I speak to shift atmospheres.
I do not speak to soothe—I speak to stir the Spirit.
I do not speak for applause—I speak for impact!

Wise words bring many benefits. — Proverbs 12:14 (NLT)

I Speak to Heal—Not to Harm

This **Battle Cry** makes a restorative declaration. It is a vivid contrast-**reckless speech wounds, but wise words mend**. It's a call to wield **language as a healing force**, especially for legacy, ministry, and covenant relationships.

I do not wield reckless words—*I carry the tongue of the wise!*
I do not speak to wound—*I speak to restore!*
I do not pierce with poison—*I cut through chaos with compassion!*

Let the reckless fall silent—*their words are daggers without aim!*
Let the wise rise up—*our tongues are tools of healing and hope!*
Let every sentence be a salve—*every phrase a fortress of peace!*

I speak with precision—*my words mend what swords have torn!*
I speak with purpose—*my voice is a balm to the broken!*
I speak with power—*my tongue turns battlefields into sanctuaries!*

I do not echo destruction—*I declare restoration!*
I do not stir strife—*I summon strength!*
I do not provoke pain—*I prophesy peace!*
My mouth is not a weapon of recklessness—*it is a wellspring of healing!*
My speech is not careless—*it is crafted in the fire of wisdom!*
My voice is not loud—*it is loaded with life!*

So I cry out with holy defiance:
I will not speak to destroy—I speak to deliver!
I will not pierce with pride—I heal with humility!
I will not echo recklessness—I roar with redemption!

Let every reckless word be silenced.
Let every wise tongue rise with healing.
Let every voice be a vessel of restoration.

This is my battle cry *I speak with the sword of wisdom and the shield of healing!*
I do not speak to strike—I speak to save.
I do not speak to divide—I speak to deliver.
I do not speak for noise—I speak for nations!

The words of the reckless pierce like swords, but the tongue of the wise brings healing. — Proverbs 12:18 (NIV)

I Guard My Mouth—My Life is Secured!

> This is a **Battle Cry** that makes a bold declaration of spiritual discipline, legacy protection, and generational wisdom. It is a powerful warning and a covenant invitation; that **guarded speech is life-giving, while reckless words invite destruction.**

I do not speak without aim—*I guard my mouth like a fortress!*
I do not unleash reckless words—*I seal my lips with wisdom!*
I do not open wide to ruin—*I speak only what builds, blesses, and breaks chains!*

My silence is strength—not surrender.
My restraint is power—not passivity.
My guarded mouth is a gate of life—not a door to destruction!

I do not speak to impress—*I speak to preserve!*
I do not speak to provoke—*I speak to protect!*
I do not speak to be loud—*I speak to be led!*

My lips are not loose—they are *locked with discernment!*
My tongue is not untamed—*it is trained by truth!*
My voice is not reckless—*it is ruled by righteousness!*

I guard my mouth like a warrior guards his sword.
I speak with intention, not impulse.
I preserve my life with every word I choose not to say.

So I cry out with fierce conviction:
I will not be ruined by reckless speech—I rise by righteous silence!
I will not open wide to destruction—I speak only what heaven authorizes!
I will not be a mouthpiece of chaos—
I am a messenger of life!

Let every careless tongue be quieted.
Let every guarded mouth be honored.
Let every voice be trained for triumph.

This is my battle cry *I guard my mouth, and I guard my mission!*
I do not speak to stir—I speak to strengthen.
I do not speak to ruin—I speak to reign.
I do not speak for reaction—I speak for revelation!

The one who guards his mouth preserves his life; the one who opens wide his lips comes to ruin.
— Proverbs 13:3 (NASB)

I Speak Peace That Shatters Fury!

This is a **Battle Cry** that turns truth into a declaration of restraint and redemptive authority. This cry is a powerful reminder that **our words carry spiritual weight–either to calm storms or to ignite them.**

I do not fight with fury—*I disarm with gentleness!*
I do not stir storms—*I speak stillness into chaos!*
I do not fuel fire—*I quench it with the calm of wisdom!*

My voice is not weak—*it is a weapon of peace!*
My answer is not passive—*it is a force that turns wrath away!*
My tone is not timid—*it is tempered by truth and trained for triumph!*

I do not provoke—*I pacify with power!*
I do not lash out—*I lead with light!*
I do not stir up anger—*I speak with authority that settles storms!*

My words are not harsh—*they are healing!*
My speech is not reckless—*it is redeeming!*
My tongue is not wild—*it is wise and Spirit-led!*

I am not a voice of rage—*I am a vessel of restoration!*
I do not echo wrath—*I echo the heart of heaven!*
I do not speak to win arguments—*I speak to win souls!*

So I cry out with holy resolve:
I will not stir up anger—I will silence it with gentleness!
I will not speak to inflame—I will speak to transform!
I will not answer with heat—I will answer with healing!

Let every harsh word fall to the ground.
Let every gentle answer rise like a shield.
Let every voice be trained to turn wrath into wisdom.

This is my battle cry *I speak peace that pierces fury!*
I do not shout to conquer—I whisper to calm.
I do not speak to stir—I speak to still.
I do not fight with fire—I fight with the breath of heaven!

A gentle answer turns away wrath, but a harsh word stirs up anger. — Proverbs 15:1 (NASB)

I Speak What Heaven Commends—Not What Folly Demands

> This is a **Battle Cry** that honors the power of wise speech and the sacred responsibility of carrying truth. It is a declaration of discernment and spiritual authority, especially in a world flooded with noise.

I do not speak to impress—*I speak to instruct!*
I do not echo foolishness—*I release knowledge with fire and focus!*
I do not pour out noise—*I pour out truth that pierces the dark!*

My tongue is trained in truth—*not twisted in folly!*
My mouth is a messenger of wisdom—*not a megaphone of confusion!*
My voice carries clarity—*not chaos!*

I commend knowledge with every word.
I carry revelation in every phrase.
I speak not from ego—I speak from encounter!

I do not babble—*I build!*
I do not rant—*I reveal!*
I do not speak to stir—*I speak to strengthen!*

My tongue is a torch—*lighting the path of understanding!*
My speech is sacred—*set apart for truth!*
My voice is victorious—*because it carries heaven's wisdom!*

So I cry out with unwavering fire:
I will not speak folly—I will speak fire-tested knowledge!
I will not echo fools—I will declare what the wise
commend!
I will not pour out confusion—I will pour out clarity!

Let every foolish mouth be silenced.
Let every wise tongue rise with truth.
Let every voice be a vessel of divine insight.

This is my battle cry ⚔ *I speak what builds, not
what breaks!*
I do not speak to entertain—I speak to enlighten.
I do not speak to be heard—I speak to be heeded.
I do not speak for noise—I speak for nations!

The tongue of the wise commends knowledge, but the
mouths of fools pour out folly. — Proverbs 15:2 (ESV)

My Tongue Bears Life—Not Brokeness!

This is a **Battle Cry** that makes truth into a generational anthem of restoration. It is a perfect foundation for a declaration that speaks to healing and the sacred power of speech.

I do not speak to crush—*I speak to cultivate!*
I do not twist truth—*I release words rooted in righteousness!*
I do not break spirits—*I build them with the breath of life!*

My tongue is not twisted—*it is tethered to truth!*
My speech is not perverse—*it is pure and powerful!*
My voice is not reckless—*it is a refuge for the weary!*

I speak gently—but my gentleness shakes strongholds.
I speak softly—but my softness splits stone hearts.
I speak life—and life rises like a tree from every word I sow!

I do not speak to wound—*I speak to water!*
I do not speak to tear down—*I speak to lift up!*
I do not speak to break—*I speak to bloom!*

My tongue is a tree of life—*its fruit heals, its shade restores!*
My words are seeds of strength—*planted in broken ground!*
My voice is a river of renewal—*flowing from the throne of grace!*

So I cry out with holy fire:
I will not break the spirit—I will breathe life into it!
I will not speak perverseness—I will speak purity!
I will not twist truth—I will plant it deep and watch it
rise!

Let every perverse tongue be silenced.
Let every gentle voice rise like a forest of healing.
Let every word be a branch of restoration.

This is my battle cry ⸺ *I speak life, and life
takes root!*
I do not speak to destroy—I speak to deliver.
I do not speak to curse—I speak to cultivate.
I do not speak for pride—I speak for purpose!

A gentle tongue is a tree of life, but perverseness in it breaks
the spirit. — Proverbs 15:4 (ESV)

I Speak with Precision—Because My Heart is Anchored in Wisdom!

This is a **Battle Cry** that honors the godly heart. A heart that guards its words like treasures and releases them like arrows of truth. **It is a beautiful invitation to pause, discern, and speak from a place of spiritual authority.**

I do not speak on impulse—*I speak from intention!*
I do not react—*I respond with revelation!*
I do not rush to speak—*I pause to hear heaven!*

My words are not wild—*they are weighed in the fire of discernment!*
My tongue is not untamed—*it is trained by truth and tempered by grace!*
My voice is not careless—*it is carved from the counsel of the Spirit!*

I think before I speak—because my words carry weight.
I pause before I declare—because my voice shifts atmospheres.
I listen before I launch—because my heart is aligned with heaven!

I do not speak to be clever—*I speak to be clear!*
I do not speak to be loud—*I speak to be led!*
I do not speak to stir—*I speak to strengthen!*

My heart is a chamber of wisdom—*every word is forged in its fire!*
My mouth is a gate of glory—*opened only by divine prompting!*
My speech is sacred—*because it flows from a consecrated core!*

So I cry out with holy resolve:
**I will not speak without thought—I speak with thunderous
clarity!**
I will not release empty words—I release divine strategy!
I will not echo emotion—I declare eternal truth!

Let every reckless voice be quieted.
Let every godly heart rise with careful speech.
Let every word be a weapon of wisdom.

This is my battle cry *I speak from the stillness of
strength!*
I do not speak to react—I speak to redeem.
I do not speak to impress—I speak to impact.
I do not speak from impulse—I speak from intimacy with God!

The heart of the godly thinks carefully before speaking.
— Proverbs 15:28 (NLT)

BATTLE CRIES

For
Peace

BATTLE CRY

Peace Is My Weapon, Gratitude Is My Banner

> This is a **Battle Cry of peace**, to carry authority, unity, and gratitude into every spiritual confrontation. It's not passive, it's a declaration that peace is a weapon, a mantle, and a ruling force.

Let the peace of Christ rule—
not visit, not whisper,
but **govern** my heart like a roaring King.

I declare
Peace is not weakness—it is warfare wrapped in stillness.
Peace is not retreat—it is the authority to stand unshaken.
Peace is not silence—it is the voice of heaven saying, "Be still and know."

I do not bow to chaos.
I do not serve anxiety.
I do not answer to fear.

I am ruled by peace.
I am called to unity.
I am marked by gratitude.

I rise with this cry:
— Let peace crush every storm.
— Let unity silence division.
— Let thanksgiving unlock the gates of heaven.

I am a warrior of calm in the middle of battle.
I am a peacemaker with fire in my bones.
I am a member of one body—called to walk in harmony,
to fight with grace,
to reign with peace.

So I lift my voice:
Peace rules here.
Gratitude reigns here.
Christ is King here.

And I will not be moved.

Let the peace of Christ rule in your hearts, since as members of one body you were called to peace. And be thankful.
— Colossians 3:15 (ESV)

I Bear the Fruit of Fire

This is a fierce, Spirit-empowered **Battle Cry** that is a declaration that the fruit of the Spirit is not soft or passive, but a blazing standard of divine authority and unshakable identity.

I do not fight with fists—I war with fruit.
I do not conquer with rage—I reign with Spirit.

Love is my sword.
Joy is my roar.
Peace is my shield.
Forbearance is my stance.
Kindness is my strike.
Goodness is my banner.
Faithfulness is my flame.

I declare
Love that breaks chains and burns through hate.
Joy that thunders louder than despair.
Peace that silences storms and commands stillness.
Forbearance that outlasts every attack.
Kindness that disarms the enemy with grace.
Goodness that exposes darkness with light.
Faithfulness that never retreats, never folds, never dies.

I am not weak—I am Spirit-forged.
I am not soft—I am heaven-tempered.
I am not alone—I am filled, sealed, and sent.
So I rise with fire in my bones and fruit in my hands.

I fight with the evidence of heaven.
I war with the character of Christ.
I conquer with the Spirit of the Living God.

This is my cry:
I bear fruit that breaks strongholds.
I bear fruit that builds legacies.
I bear fruit that cannot be stolen.
I bear fruit that will not rot.
I bear fruit that multiplies in battle.

Let the enemy tremble—
for I do not fight alone.
I fight filled.
I fight fierce.
I fight fruitful.

But the fruit of the Spirit is love, joy, peace, forbearance, kindness, goodness, faithfulness. — Galatians 5:22 (ESV)

I Am Set Apart to See the Lord

This is a **Battle Cry of holiness**–fierce, uncompromising, and radiant with the authority. It's not just a call to purity–it's a declaration of spiritual visibility, legacy, and divine fire:

I do not blend in.
I do not bow to compromise.
I do not walk the wide road.

I am set apart.
I am marked by fire.
I am clothed in holiness.

I declare
Holiness is not perfection—it is pursuit.
Holiness is not distance—it is devotion.
Holiness is not silence—it is the sound of heaven roaring
through me.

I make every effort—
to live in peace,
to walk in purity,
to stand in the light.

I do not settle for shadows.
I do not trade truth for comfort.
I do not dilute the call.

**Without holiness, no one will see the Lord—
and I was born to see Him.
I was born to reflect Him.
I was born to reveal Him.**

So I rise with this cry
— Let holiness burn away every lie.
— Let peace disarm every division.
— Let purity unlock divine vision.

I am not afraid to be different.
I am not ashamed to be consecrated.
I am not silent about the fire within.

**I am holy—not hidden.
I am holy—not passive.
I am holy—not alone.**

I walk in peace.
I war in purity.
I live to see the Lord.

Make every effort to live in peace with everyone and to be holy; without holiness no one will see the Lord.
— Hebrews 12:14 (ESV)

BATTLE CRY

I Chase Peace, I Wield Goodness, I Turn from the Dark

> This is a **Battle Cry** of righteous pursuit, a declaration that holiness is active, peace is hunted, and goodness is a weapon of light.

I do not drift—I turn.
I do not wait—I pursue.
I do not hide—I rise.

I turn from evil with fire in my eyes.
I do good with thunder in my hands.
I seek peace like a warrior hunts victory.

I declare
Evil will not write my story.
Goodness is my sword, forged in obedience.
Peace is not passive—it is a prize worth chasing.

I do not flirt with darkness.
I do not entertain compromise.
I do not walk in circles.

I pivot with purpose.
I pursue with passion.
I fight with goodness.

Let the enemy tremble—
for I am not just avoiding evil,

I am **running toward righteousness.**

I chase peace through conflict.
I chase peace through forgiveness.
I chase peace through truth.

This is my cry
— I turn from what corrupts.
— I do what restores.
— I seek what reconciles.
— I pursue what heals.

I am not neutral—I am **holy on the move.**
I am not quiet—I am **goodness unleashed.**
I am not still—I am **peace in pursuit.**

And I will not stop
until the darkness flees,
until goodness reigns,
until peace is planted
in every heart, every home, every generation.

They must turn from evil and do good; they must seek peace
and pursue it. — 1 Peter 3:11 (ESV)

I Sow Peace to Reap Righteousness

This is a **Battle Cry of sacred urgency**. A declaration that peacemaking is not passive, but a divine strategy for unleashing righteousness across families, communities, and legacies.

This is no small call.
This is no quiet task.
This is **holy warfare**.

I am a peacemaker—
not a peacekeeper,
not a bystander,
but a sower of heaven's justice.

I declare
Peace is my seed.
Righteousness is my harvest.
Every act of peace is a strike against chaos.

I do not sow in fear.
I do not sow in silence.
I do not sow for applause.

I sow in peace—
with urgency,
with fire,
with vision.

I sow into conflict.
I sow into brokenness.
I sow into generations not yet born.

Because I know:
— What I plant today will rise tomorrow.
— What I water with grace will bloom in power.
— What I sow in peace will reap a harvest that shakes
nations.

This is my cry
I will not delay.
I will not shrink back.
I will not forget the weight of this call.

I sow peace like arrows into the soil.
I sow peace like fire into the future.
I sow peace like legacy into the land.

And I will reap righteousness—
not just for me,
but for my children,
for my community,
for the kingdom.

I am a peacemaker.
I am a sower.
I am a harvester of heaven.

Peacemakers who sow in peace reap a harvest of
righteousness. — James 3:18 (ESV)

Guard Me, O Peace of God

This is a **heartfelt, Spirit-breathed Battle Cry for peace.** It speaks into the ache, the chaos, and the longing–and to declare that peace is not just a promise, but a fortress built by God Himself

I am not asking for escape.
I am crying out for **peace that fights for me.**

Not the peace the world offers—
thin, fleeting, conditional.
But the peace of God—
unshakable, unexplainable, undefeated.

I declare
Let peace rise like a shield around my heart.
Let peace stand like a sentry over my mind.
Let peace roar louder than anxiety, fear, and confusion.

I do not need to understand.
I need to be **held.**
I need to be **guarded.**
I need to be **kept** in the refuge of Christ.

So I cry out:
— Guard me when the storm rages.
— Guard me when the silence screams.
— Guard me when the battle is within.

Peace is not passive—it is a warrior.
Peace is not quiet—it is a command.
Peace is not fragile—it is forged in Christ.

I will not be ruled by chaos.
I will not be led by fear.
I will not be broken by the unknown.

I am guarded.
I am covered.
I am kept—by the peace of God.

And I will stand,
not because I understand,
but because I am held.

And the peace of God, which transcends all understanding,
will guard your hearts and your minds in Christ Jesus.
— Philippians 4:7 (ESV)

I Choose Joy, I Wage Peace

This is a bold, beautiful **Battle Cry** for joy—one that confronts deceit, honors peacemaking, and declares joy as a divine inheritance. It speaks in spiritual authority and emotional resilience.

I see the schemes.
I hear the whispers.
I feel the tension in the air.

But I do not bow to deceit.
I do not partner with fear.
I do not echo the chaos.

**I am a peacemaker—
and joy is my reward.**

I declare
I sow peace into conflict.
I speak peace into confusion.
I carry peace into every room I enter.

And because I promote peace,
joy rises in me like a river.
Not shallow. Not circumstantial.
But deep, defiant, and divine.

I do not wait for joy to find me.
I fight for it. I choose it. I wear it like armor.

Let deceit unravel.
Let evil expose itself.
Let every plot fall powerless.

Because I walk in truth.
I walk in peace.
And I walk in **joy that cannot be stolen.**

This is my inheritance.
This is my resistance.
This is my cry:

I wage peace—
and I overflow with joy.

Deceit is in the hearts of those who plot evil, but those who promote peace have joy. — Proverbs 12:20 (ESV)

BATTLE CRY

Peace at the Gates

This is a powerful, **covenant-rooted Battle Cry** to declare divine favor, relational restoration, and the authority of walking in the Lord's pleasure. It speaks into spiritual warfare and the promise of peace even in the presence of enemies.

I Do Not Fear:

I do not fear the opposition.
I do not flinch at the gates.
I do not retreat from the tension.

**I walk in the way that pleases the Lord—
and that changes everything.**

I declare
The Lord delights in my steps.
His favor surrounds me like fire.
His pleasure is my protection.

Enemies may rise,
but they will not prevail.
They will be **disarmed by peace,
undone by mercy,**
silenced by the pleasure of God.

I do not negotiate with fear.
I do not entertain revenge.
I do not rehearse offense.

**I stand in the pleasure of the Lord—
and peace becomes my weapon.**

Let every adversary be softened.
Let every accuser be quieted.
Let every conflict be turned into covenant.

Because the Lord is pleased,
He commands peace to come.
Not just within me—
but around me,
through me,
even with those who once opposed me.

This is my cry:
Peace at the gates.
Peace with my enemies.
Peace because I walk in His way.

When the LORD takes pleasure in anyone's way, he causes
their enemies to make peace with them.
— Proverbs 16:7 (ESV)

I Choose Peace, Even When It Costs Me

This is a **Battle Cry** to honor the tension between conviction and compassion, and to declare peace as a bold, intentional act of spiritual warfare. It's designed to resonate with your legacy work, equipping others to walk in unity, restoration, and divine authority.

**I do not wait for peace to come to me.
I pursue it. I protect it. I proclaim it.**

Even when it's hard.
Even when it's misunderstood.
Even when it costs me comfort, pride, or silence.

I declare
I will not be baited by offense.
I will not be ruled by resentment.
I will not be hardened by hurt.

**I choose peace—because I am called to it.
I choose peace—because it depends on me.
I choose peace—because it reflects the heart of God.**

Let every broken bridge be offered a plank.
Let every wound be met with mercy.
Let every enemy be given a chance to become a friend.

I do not compromise truth.
I do not abandon justice.
But I do **fight for peace**—with courage, with humility,
with love.

This is my cry:
**As far as it depends on me—
I will live at peace.
I will sow peace.
I will be peace.**

Because peace is not passive.
Peace is not weak.
Peace is the path of the bold,
and the blessing of the faithful.

If it is possible, as far as it depends on you, live at peace with
everyone. — Romans 12:18 (ESV)

I Turn, I Rise, I Pursue

This is a fierce **Battle Cry** to confront darkness, declare righteousness, and charge forward in relentless pursuit of peace. It's designed to resonate with your legacy calling, equipping warriors of faith to rise with clarity, conviction, and covenant authority.

I do not flirt with compromise.
I do not entertain shadows.
I do not stand still in the face of evil.

I turn.
I rise.
I pursue.

I declare
I turn from every lie, every lure, every lesser thing.
I rise into righteousness—bold, blazing, unashamed.
I pursue peace like a warrior chasing victory.

Peace is not passive.
It is not polite.
It is not optional.

Peace is a mission.
Peace is a mantle.
Peace is a fight worth waging.

I do good—not to be seen,
but to be aligned with heaven.
I seek peace—not to avoid conflict, but to conquer it with truth.

Let evil fall behind me.
Let goodness blaze before me.
Let peace be the path I carve with every step.

This is my cry:
I turn from evil.
I do what is right.
I seek peace—and I will not stop until it reigns.

Because I am not just a peacemaker—
I am a peace pursuer.
And I will not be denied.

Turn from evil and do good; seek peace and pursue it.
— Psalm 34:14 (ESV)

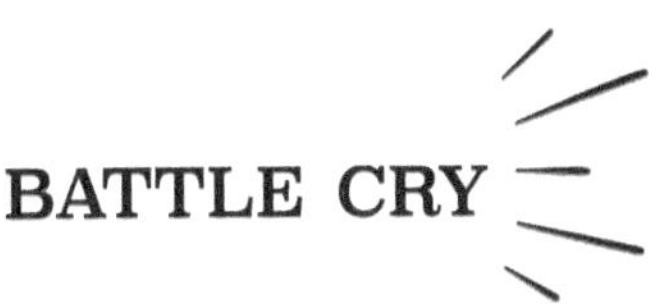

I Bless Where Others Curse

This is a **Battle Cry** that carries the weight of heaven's justice and the tenderness of heaven's mercy. It's a fierce, counter-cultural declaration to equip warriors of faith to respond with blessing, speak with integrity, and pursue peace as a divine inheritance.

I do not mirror darkness.
I do not echo insult.
I do not repay evil with evil.

**I am called to bless—
and I will not be silent.**

I declare
I bless when I'm wounded.
I bless when I'm betrayed.
I bless when the world expects retaliation.

Because I am not ruled by reaction—
I am governed by grace.

I guard my tongue like a sword of light.
I speak truth without venom.
I turn from evil—not in weakness, but in holy defiance.

I do good—not to earn favor,
but to reflect the One who called me.
I seek peace—not to avoid battle,

but to win it with blessing.
Let every insult fall powerless.
Let every curse be reversed.
Let every evil be met with heaven's mercy.

This is my cry:
I bless where others curse.
I speak life where others tear down.
I pursue peace—and I inherit blessing.

Because I was not called to echo the world—
I was called to transform it.

Do not repay evil with evil or insult with insult. On the contrary, repay evil with blessing, because to this you were called so that you may inherit a blessing. For, "Whoever would love life and see good days must keep their tongue from evil and their lips from deceitful speech. They must turn from evil and do good; they must seek peace and pursue it." — 1 Peter 3:9–11 (ESV)

I Stand in the Unshakable

This **Battle Cry** is a thunderous declaration of **God's unshakable love and covenantal power**–a cry that defies instability and declares divine permanence. It's a **fierce Battle Cry of immovable love and unstoppable peace**, for warriors who stand in compassion and conquer through covenant.

Let the earth quake.
Let the mountains crumble.
Let the hills fall away.

I do not flinch.
I do not flee.
I do not forget who holds me.

I declare
His love is unfailing—it cannot be shaken.
His peace is covenant—it cannot be revoked.
His compassion is fierce—it cannot be silenced.

I am not anchored in terrain—I am anchored in truth.
I am not held by circumstance—I am held by covenant.
I am not defined by chaos—I am defined by compassion.

Even if the mountains fall—He remains.
Even if the hills vanish—His peace stands.
Even if all else fails—His love does not.

This is my cry:
— I stand in the unshakable.
— I war from the immovable.
— I rise in the eternal.

The covenant holds.
The peace reigns.
The love endures.

I am not shaken—I am sealed.
I am not removed—I am restored.
I am not forsaken—I am fiercely loved.

Because He said it—
I believe it.
I declare it.
I live it.

And I will not be moved.

"Though the mountains be shaken and the hills be removed, yet my unfailing love for you will not be shaken nor my covenant of peace be removed," says the LORD, who has compassion on you. — Isaiah 54:10 (ESV)

BATTLE CRIES

For
Forgiveness

I Lead with Kindness—I Fight with Forgiveness!

This is the **Battle Cry** of a warrior who chooses compassion over cruelty, tenderness over retaliation, and forgiveness as a weapon of heaven. It's a declaration that **love is not weakness, it's warfare.**

I do not harden—I *stay tenderhearted!*
I do not retaliate—I *release forgiveness!*
I do not carry offense—I *carry the cross of Christ!*

Kindness is my strategy—*not silence, but strength!*
Forgiveness is my weapon—*not surrender, but spiritual victory!*
Tenderness is my armor—*not fragility, but fierce grace!*

I declare
I will not be bitter—I will *be bold in mercy!*
I will not be cold—I will *be clothed in compassion!*
I will not be stuck in pain—I will *walk free in forgiveness!*

I forgive because I've been forgiven.
I love because I've been loved.
I fight with grace—*because grace won the war for me!*

So I cry out with holy humility and divine fire:
I lead with kindness—I fight with forgiveness!
I will not be hardened—I will be healed!
I will not echo offense—I will echo Christ!

Let anger rise—I answer with tenderness.
Let offense linger—I respond with release.
Let division threaten—I roar: *"I choose love, and I win with grace!"*

THIS IS MY BATTLE CRY—
I do not just survive conflict—I transform it with compassion!
I do not just endure pain—I redeem it with forgiveness!
I do not just speak peace—I live it with power!
As Christ forgave me—I forgive, I love, I lead!

Be kind to one another, tenderhearted, forgiving one another, as God in Christ forgave you. — Ephesians 4:32 (ESV)

BATTLE CRY

I Forgive in Prayer—I Fight for Heaven's Flow!

> This **Battle Cry** is for the warrior who refuses to let offense block heaven's power. It's a declaration that forgiveness is not optional–it's essential for divine release.
>
> Prayer becomes warfare when forgiveness clears the way.

I do not pray with clenched fists—I *open my hands to forgive!*
I do not carry grudges into battle—I *drop them at the altar!*
I do not let offense speak louder than obedience—I *choose release over revenge!*

My prayers are not hindered—they are *heaven-fueled!*
My heart is not divided—it is *wholly surrendered!*
My spirit is not clogged with bitterness—it is *cleansed by mercy!*

I declare
I forgive *before I ask.*
I release *before I receive.*
I let go *so heaven can flow!*

I will not let unforgiveness block my breakthrough.
I will not let offense silence my authority.
I will not let bitterness build walls between me and God.

So I cry out with fierce humility and holy resolve:
I forgive in prayer—I fight for heaven's flow!

I will not hold back—I will release and rise!
I will not be bound—I will be bold in mercy!

Let wounds whisper—*I answer with release.*
Let offense echo—*I respond with obedience.*
Let pride resist—I roar: *"I forgive, and heaven responds!"*

THIS IS MY BATTLE CRY—
I do not just pray—I purge the poison!
I do not just speak—I surrender the sword of offense!
I do not just ask—I align with heaven's heart!
As I forgive—my Father forgives me, and the heavens open wide!

And whenever you stand praying, forgive, if you have anything against anyone, so that your Father also who is in heaven may forgive you your trespasses. — Mark 11:25 (ESV)

I Confess—I Am Cleansed!

This is the **Battle Cry** of a warrior who refuses to hide in shame or silence. It's a declaration that confession is not weakness, it's the gateway to cleansing, restoration, and divine justice. The battlefield is not just external–it's the heart, and this warrior fights with truth.

I do not conceal—I confess *with courage!*
I do not justify—I surrender *with boldness!*
I do not run from guilt—I *run to grace!*

I declare
My sin is not my sentence—*my confession is my freedom!*
My past is not my prison—*my cleansing is complete!*
My shame is not my story—*my Savior is faithful and just!*

I fight with honesty—*no mask, no fear!*
I stand in mercy—*no stain too deep!*
I rise in righteousness—*no failure too final!*

So I cry out with holy defiance and fierce surrender:
I confess—I am cleansed!
I expose the darkness—and light floods in!
I lay down my guilt—and I rise in grace!

Let accusation roar—I answer with repentance.
Let shame linger—I respond with truth.
Let regret haunt—I roar: *"I am forgiven, I am free, I am clean!"*

THIS IS MY BATTLE CRY—
I do not just admit—I activate heaven's justice!
I do not just repent—I receive divine cleansing!
I do not just speak—I step into restoration!
He is faithful—He is just—He has forgiven me, and I fight
from freedom!

If we confess our sins, he is faithful and just to forgive us our sins and cleanse us from all unrighteousness. —1 John 1:9 (ESV)

I Forgive Without Limit—I Fight With Endless Grace!

> This is the **Battle Cry** of a warrior who refuses to count offenses but chooses to multiply mercy. It's a declaration that forgiveness is not a quota–it's a lifestyle of spiritual strength. This warrior doesn't keep score, they keep surrendering.

I do not measure—I *move in mercy!*
I do not tally wounds—I *release with resolve!*
I do not grow weary—I *grow deeper in grace!*

I forgive again—*and again—and again!*
I fight bitterness with *relentless compassion!*
I battle offense with *unshakable obedience!*

I declare ⊶—
I will not be hardened—I will *be holy!*
I will not be petty—I will *be powerful in grace!*
I will not be stuck in cycles—I will *break them with forgiveness!*

My strength is not in retaliation—it's in restoration.
My victory is not in vengeance—it's in virtue.
My legacy is not in keeping score—it's in keeping peace.

So I cry out with fierce mercy and divine endurance:
I forgive without limit—I fight with endless grace!
I will not count offenses—I will count on God!
I will not grow cold—I will grow bold in love!

Let betrayal repeat—I answer with release.
Let offense multiply—I respond with multiplied mercy.
Let bitterness knock—I roar: *"I forgive again—and heaven backs me every time!"*

THIS IS MY BATTLE CRY—
I do not just endure—I overcome with grace!
I do not just survive—I sow mercy that multiplies!
I do not just forgive—I forge a legacy of love!
Seventy-seven times? I go beyond—because grace never quits!

Then Peter came up and said to him, "Lord, how often will my brother sin against me, and I forgive him? As many as seven times?" Jesus said to him, "I do not say to you seven times, but seventy-seven times." — Matthew 18:21-22 (ESV)

BATTLE CRY

I Forgive to Be Free—I Release to Be Restored!

This is the **Battle Cry** of a warrior who understands that forgiveness is not optional–it's essential. It's a declaration that mercy is a two-edged sword: when we extend it, we receive it. **This warrior fights not with grudges, but with grace.**

I do not chain myself with offense—*I break free with forgiveness!*
I do not block heaven's mercy—*I open the floodgates with release!*
I do not hold others hostage—*I choose freedom for all, including me!*
I forgive—*because I need forgiveness!*
I release—*because I refuse to be bound!*
I let go—*because I long to be lifted by grace!*

I declare

I will not trade mercy for pride—*I choose humility and healing!*
I will not cling to pain—*I will cling to the cross!*
I will not deny others grace—*I will walk in the fullness of it!*

Forgiveness is my weapon.
Mercy is my mantle.
Restoration is my reward—and *I fight for it with every release!*

So I cry out with holy urgency and fierce surrender:
I forgive to be free—I release to be restored!
I will not block heaven—I will open my heart!
I will not hold back—I will let go and rise!

Let offense whisper—I answer with obedience.
Let bitterness linger—I respond with bold mercy.
Let pride resist—I roar: *"I forgive—because I need
forgiveness too!"*

THIS IS MY BATTLE CRY—
I do not just speak grace—I live it out loud!
I do not just ask for mercy—I extend it without hesitation!
I do not just fight for justice—I fight for reconciliation!
Forgiveness is my freedom—and I will not let it slip away!

For if you forgive others their trespasses, your heavenly
Father will also forgive you, but if you do not forgive
others their trespasses, neither will your Father forgive your
trespasses. — Matthew 6:14-15 (ESV)

I Lay Down Judgment—I Rise in Mercy!

This **Battle Cry** is for the warrior who refuses to wield condemnation as a weapon. It's a declaration of spiritual authority rooted in humility, mercy, and the power of forgiveness.

I do not judge—*I release!*
I do not condemn—*I cover in grace!*
I do not retaliate—*I forgive and rise!*

I declare
I will not be a gatekeeper of shame—*I am a herald of healing!*
I will not be a voice of accusation—*I am a vessel of compassion!*
I will not echo the world's harshness—*I speak heaven's mercy!*

Judgment is not my sword—*mercy is my mantle!*
Condemnation is not my cry—*forgiveness is my roar!*
I do not tear down—*I build up with grace!*

I choose the high ground of humility.
I walk the narrow path of mercy.
I wield the weapon of forgiveness—and *I fight for freedom!*

So I cry out with fierce resolve and holy surrender:
I lay down judgment—I rise in mercy!
I silence condemnation—I speak life!
I forgive—because I am forgiven!
Let the accuser rage—I answer with grace.

Let bitterness beckon—I respond with blessing.
Let pride provoke—I roar: *"I choose mercy over might!"*

THIS IS MY BATTLE CRY—
I do not fight to punish—I fight to restore.
I do not stand to accuse—I stand to redeem.
I do not war with wrath—I war with love.
I am a warrior of grace—and I will not be moved!

Judge not, and you will not be judged; condemn not, and
you will not be condemned; forgive, and you will be forgiven.
— Luke 6:37 (ESV)

I Bear the Burden—I Break the Cycle!

> This is the cry of a warrior who refuses to let offense fracture unity. It's a bold declaration that forgiveness is not weakness–it's warfare. To bear with one another is to fight for peace, and to forgive is to mirror the mercy of the King.

I bear the weight of grace—*not the chains of complaint!*
I carry the mantle of mercy—*not the burden of bitterness!*
I forgive—*because I am forgiven!*
I release—*because I am redeemed!*
I do not retaliate—*I reconcile!*
I do not rehearse the wound—I restore the bond!
I do not echo offense—I answer with obedience!

I declare

I will not let complaint become my compass—*I follow the way of Christ!*
I will not let division define me—*I fight for unity with every breath!*
I will not let pain speak louder than purpose—*I roar with redemption!*

Forgiveness is my shield.
Compassion is my armor.
Restoration is my mission—and *I will not retreat!*

So I cry out with fierce love and holy resolve:
I bear the burden—I break the cycle!

I forgive as I've been forgiven!
I fight for unity—I war with grace!

Let complaint rise—I answer with compassion.
Let offense linger—I respond with release.
Let pride resist—I roar: *"I will not be ruled by resentment!"*

THIS IS MY BATTLE CRY—
I do not just endure—I embrace with mercy!
I do not just survive—I restore with strength!
I do not just forgive—I forge peace with fire!
I am a warrior of reconciliation—and I will not be moved!

Bearing with one another and, if one has a complaint against another, forgiving each other; as the Lord has forgiven you, so you also must forgive. — Colossians 3:13 (ESV)

I Cancel the Debt—I Claim the Mercy!

This is the **Battle Cry** of a warrior who understands that forgiveness is not a transaction–it's transformation. It's a declaration that we release others not because they deserve it, but because we've been released by the blood of the Lamb.

I do not tally wrongs—*I tear up the ledger!*
I do not demand repayment—*I declare freedom!*
I forgive—*because I've been forgiven!*
I release—*because I've been redeemed!*

I cancel the debt of offense—*because mine was canceled at the cross!*
I do not hold others hostage—*I walk free and set others free!*
I do not cling to what's owed—*I cling to what was paid in full!*

I declare
I will not be a keeper of grudges—*I am a carrier of grace!*
I will not be a collector of pain—*I am a releaser of peace!*
I will not be a prisoner of pride—*I am a warrior of mercy!*

Forgiveness is my freedom.
Grace is my ground.
Mercy is my mission—*and I will not be moved!*

So I cry out with fierce surrender and holy fire:

I cancel the debt—I claim the mercy!
I forgive as I've been forgiven!
I release what's owed—I receive what's eternal!

Let guilt whisper—I answer with grace.
Let offense linger—I respond with release.
Let pride provoke—I roar: *"Paid in full—so I forgive in full!"*

THIS IS MY BATTLE CRY—
I do not fight to settle scores—I fight to set captives free.
I do not war with wrath—I war with mercy.
I do not demand justice—I declare grace.
I am a warrior of forgiveness—and I will not be shaken!

And forgive us our debts, as we also have forgiven our debtors. — Matthew 6:12 (ESV)

BATTLE CRY

I Repent—I Rise—I Receive!

> This is the **Battle Cry** of a warrior who steps into the battlefield not with shame, but with surrender. It's a declaration of transformation: repentance is the doorway, baptism is the burial of the old, and the Holy Spirit is the fire that fuels the new.

I do not hide—*I repent!*
I do not delay—*I step into the waters!*
I do not walk alone—*I receive the Spirit of power!*

I lay down sin—*I rise in salvation!*
I bury the old—*I emerge reborn!*
I receive the gift—*I carry the flame!*

I declare
I will not be defined by my past—*I am marked by mercy!*
I will not be bound by guilt—*I am baptized in grace!*
I will not walk in weakness—*I am filled with fire!*

Repentance is my turning point.
Baptism is my burial and resurrection.
The Holy Spirit is my power—and I will not be silenced!

So I cry out with holy fire and fierce surrender:
I repent—I rise—I receive!
I turn from sin—I run to the Savior!
I am washed—I am filled—I am sent!

Let shame speak—I answer with surrender.
Let fear linger—I respond with faith.
Let doubt whisper—I roar: *"I am forgiven, filled, and fearless!"*

THIS IS MY BATTLE CRY—
I do not just confess—I consecrate!
I do not just turn—I transform!
I do not just receive—I release the fire!
I am a warrior of the Spirit—and I will not be moved!

Jesus is my King!

And Peter said to them, "Repent and be baptized every one of you in the name of Jesus Christ for the forgiveness of your sins, and you will receive the gift of the Holy Spirit."
— Acts 2:38 (ESV)

BATTLE CRY

I Am Redeemed—I Am Released—I Am Rich in Grace!

I do not fight for approval—*I stand in redemption!*
I do not carry shame—*I am covered in blood-bought grace!*
I do not beg for mercy—*I walk in the riches of it!*

I am redeemed—*by the blood of the Lamb!*
I am forgiven—*every trespass erased!*
I am rich—*in grace that never runs dry!*

I declare

I will not be defined by failure—*I am marked by mercy!*
I will not be bound by guilt—*I am loosed by love!*
I will not walk in lack—*I overflow with grace!*

His blood is my banner.
His forgiveness is my freedom.
His grace is my ground—and I will not be shaken!

So I cry out with holy confidence and fierce gratitude:
I am redeemed—I am released—I am rich in grace!
I fight from victory—not for it!
I stand forgiven, fearless, and full!

Let accusation rise—I answer with the blood.
Let shame whisper—I respond with grace.
Let doubt linger—I roar: *"I am redeemed—and I will not retreat!"*

THIS IS MY BATTLE CRY—
I do not just survive—I stand secure!
I do not just hope—I declare truth!
I do not just receive—I release grace to others!
I am a warrior of redemption—and I will not be moved!

In him we have redemption through his blood, the forgiveness of our trespasses, according to the riches of his grace. — Ephesians 1:7 (ESV)

BATTLE CRIES

For
Your Marriage

BATTLE CRY

I Was Not Made to Stand Alone—I Was Designed for Covenant Strength!

This is a **Battle Cry of divine design, covenant partnership, and purposeful companionship.** A cry that declares *aloneness is not the final word, and that God Himself crafts helpers who are fit, fierce, and faithful. This is the anthem of warriors who recognize that partnership is power, and that help is holy.*

I do not fight in isolation—*I was made for partnership!*
I do not walk without help—*I receive what heaven has crafted!*
I do not settle for less—*I honor the one fit for me!*

I declare

Aloneness is not my portion—*God saw and answered!*
Help is not weakness—*it is divine strategy!*
Fit does not mean perfect—*it means purposefully aligned!*

This is my cry:
I was not made to stand alone—I was designed for covenant strength!
I do not reject the gift—I rise with the helper God has given!
I do not diminish her worth—I honor her as heaven's answer!

Let isolation fall—*I am joined in purpose!*
Let pride break—*I am strengthened by unity!*
Let confusion die—*I am clear in design and destiny!*

I cry this over my children:
You are not called to loneliness—*you are called to covenant!*
You are not called to independence alone—*you are called to interdependence in strength!*
You are not called to wander—*you are called to walk with the one God has fit for you!*

So I rise and declare:
We walk in unity.
We fight in partnership.
We build with help.
We reflect heaven's design.

We are the joined—
Crafted by God,
Strengthened by covenant,
Unshaken in purpose!

Then the Lord God said, "It is not good that the man should be alone; I will make him a helper fit for him."
— Genesis 2:18 (ESV)

We Are One Flesh—Joined by God—Unbreakable by Man!

This is a **Battle Cry of divine union, covenant protection, and unbreakable oneness.** A cry that declares marriage is God's creation, oneness is sacred, and no force on earth can tear apart what heaven has joined. This is the anthem of warriors who fight for unity, guard their covenant, and honor the fusion of flesh and spirit.

I do not question the design—*I honor the Creator's blueprint!*
I do not treat covenant lightly—*I guard it with fire!*
I do not fear division—*I stand in divine fusion!*

I declare
Male and female—*crafted by God from the beginning!*
One flesh—*not symbolic, but sacred!*
Joined by heaven—*not to be separated by man!*

This is my cry:
We are one flesh—joined by God—unbreakable by man!
I leave the past—I cleave with passion!
I do not fracture—I fuse in faith and fire!

Let confusion fall—*we are clear in design!*
Let culture break—*we are anchored in truth!*
Let division die—*we are sealed by heaven's hand!*

I cry this over my children:
You are not called to chaos—*you are called to covenant clarity!*
You are not called to temporary love—*you are called to eternal union!*
You are not called to separation—*you are called to sacred fusion!*

So I rise and declare:
We honor the design.
We protect the covenant.
We fight for oneness.
We reflect heaven's heart.

We are the fused—
One flesh,
One fire,
Unshaken in unity!

He answered, "Have you not read that he who created them from the beginning made them male and female, and said, 'Therefore a man shall leave his father and his mother and hold fast to his wife, and the two shall become one flesh'? So they are no longer two but one flesh. What therefore God has joined together, let not man separate."
— Matthew 19:4-6 (ESV)

I Honor the Covenant—I Guard the Sacred—I Fight for Purity!

This is a **Battle Cry of covenant, purity, and honor.** A cry that defends the sacred ground of marriage, declares war on compromise, and lifts high the banner of holy union. This is not just about morality, it's about spiritual warfare for legacy, protection of intimacy, and honoring what God has called sacred. It's the anthem of those who fight for fidelity, protect purity, and build homes that reflect heaven.

I do not treat marriage lightly—*I hold it in honor!*
I do not defile the sacred—*I protect what God has made holy!*
I do not compromise—*I stand for covenant with fire!*

I declare

Marriage is not just love—*it is warrior-level commitment!*
The marriage bed is not just intimacy—*it is sacred ground!*
Purity is not outdated—*it is a weapon of legacy!*

This is my cry:
I honor the covenant—I guard the sacred—I fight for purity!
I do not bow to culture—I rise with conviction!
I do not tolerate defilement—I defend what is holy!

Let adultery fall—*I am faithful in fire!*
Let immorality break—*I am pure in passion!*
Let compromise be crushed—*I am anchored in truth!*

I cry this over my children:
You are not confused—*you are called to honor!*
You are not unguarded—*you are protected by truth*!
You are not alone—*you are covered by covenant warriors!*

So I rise and declare:
We fight for fidelity.
We protect purity.
We honor marriage.
We build legacy.

We are the covenant keepers—
Fierce in love,
Faithful in battle,
Unshaken in truth!

Let marriage be held in honor among all, and let the marriage bed be undefiled, for God will judge the sexually immoral and adulterous. — Hebrews 13:4 (ESV)

I Found My Good Thing—I Guard It with Glory—I Walk in Favor!

> This is a **Battle Cry** of divine favor, covenant joy, and kingdom partnership. This isn't just about romance, it's about recognizing the gift, honoring the blessing, and **fighting to protect what God has favored**. It's a cry for husbands to rise with gratitude and strength, and for wives to stand in the fullness of their worth.

I did not stumble into love—*I found a good thing!*
I did not earn this grace—*I received favor from the Lord!*
I do not take her for granted—*I honor her as heaven's gift!*

I declare

She is not just my wife—*she is my divine reward!*
Our union is not ordinary—*it is marked by favor!*
Our love is not fragile—*it is fortified by God!*

This is my cry:
I found my good thing—I guard it with glory—I walk in favor!
I rise to protect—I lead with love—I fight for us!
I do not retreat—I stand as her shield and strength!

Let bitterness break—*I choose blessing!*
Let division fall—*I choose unity!*
Let apathy die—*I choose honor!*

I cry this over my children:
Marriage is not a burden—*it is a blessing!*
Love is not weakness—*it is warrior strength!*

Favor is not random—*it is released through covenant!*

So I rise and declare:
I cherish her.
I cover her.
I celebrate her.

We are the favored ones—
Joined by heaven,
Strengthened by grace,
Unshakable in love!

He who finds a wife finds a good thing and obtains favor from the Lord. — Proverbs 18:22 (ESV)

BATTLE CRY

I Leave—I Cleave—I Become One!

> This is a **Battle Cry** of covenant unity, sacred commitment, and generational shift. A cry that declares marriage is not just a bond, it's a becoming. This is the anthem of warriors who leave behind what was, hold to what is holy, and rise as one flesh, fused in purpose, fire, and legacy. It's a cry that honors the cost, celebrates the union, and defends the oneness.

I do not cling to the past—*I step into covenant!*
I do not divide my heart—*I hold fast with fire!*
I do not walk alone—*I become one in purpose and power!*

I declare
Leaving is not loss—*it is launching into legacy!*
Cleaving is not weakness—*it is warrior-level commitment!*
Becoming one is not blending—*it is birthing something divine!*

This is my cry:
I leave—I cleave—I become one!
I do not waver—I hold fast!
I do not fracture—I fuse in faith!

Let confusion fall—*we are united in covenant!*
Let division break—*we are one flesh, one fire, one future!*
Let culture fade—*we are anchored in heaven's design!*

I cry this over my children:
You are not called to chaos—*you are called to covenant!*
You are not meant to drift—*you are meant to unite!*

You are not just partners—*you are purpose-bearers, fused by God!*

So I rise and declare:
We leave with honor.
We cleave with strength.
We become one with fire.

We are the fused—
One flesh,
One flame,
Unshaken in covenant!

Therefore, a man shall leave his father and his mother and hold fast to his wife, and they shall become one flesh.
— Genesis 2:24 (ESV)

I Love Fiercely—I Stand in Truth—I Endure with Fire!

This is a **Battle Cry** of fierce love, not soft, sentimental love, but unyielding, truth-filled, warrior- love. This is the cry of those who choose patience over pride, kindness over control, and truth over convenience. It's the anthem of those who bear, believe, hope, and endure, because **love is not just a feeling, it's a force that fights and never fails.**

I do not love for comfort—*I love to conquer!*
I do not love to be seen—*I love to serve!*
I do not love when it's easy—*I love when it's war!*

I declare
Love is my weapon—and it never fails!
Love is my armor—and it never cracks!
Love is my legacy—and it never dies!

This is my cry:
I love fiercely—I stand in truth—I endure with fire!
I will be patient—I will be kind—I will not boast or break!
I will not be arrogant—I will not be rude—I will not insist on my own way!

Let envy fall—I choose *celebration!*
Let pride break—I choose *humility!*
Let resentment die—I choose *forgiveness!*
Let falsehood flee—*I rejoice in truth!*

I cry this over my children:

You are not weak—*you are warriors of love!*
You are not selfish—*you are servants of truth!*
You are not fragile—*you are fueled by endurance and hope!*

So I rise and declare:
We bear all things.
We believe all things.
We hope all things.
We endure all things.

We are the fierce lovers—
Unshaken by offense,
Unmoved by pride,
Unstoppable in truth!

Love is patient and kind; love does not envy or boast; it is not arrogant or rude. It does not insist on its own way; it is not irritable or resentful; it does not rejoice at wrongdoing but rejoices with the truth. Love bears all things, believes all things, hopes all things, endures all things.
— 1 Corinthians 13:4-7 (ESV)

I Honor the Gift—I Guard the Covenant—I Build with Wisdom!

This is a **Battle Cry** of divine provision, covenant honor, and wisdom in partnership. A cry that recognizes that earthly inheritance may come from men, but true **treasure is given by God**. This is the anthem of those who see marriage not just as companionship, **but as a strategic gift from heaven, a source of strength, discernment, and legacy.**

I do not boast in wealth—*I rejoice in wisdom!*
I do not chase possessions—*I cherish the gift!*
I do not take her for granted—*I recognize heaven's hand!*

I declare

Houses may be inherited—*but wisdom is divinely appointed!*
Wealth may be passed down—*but a prudent wife is heaven-sent!*
Marriage is not luck—*it is legacy wrapped in grace!*

This is my cry:
I honor the gift—I guard the covenant—I build with wisdom!
I do not measure value by riches—I measure by revelation!
I do not lead alone—I walk with the one God has given!

Let pride fall—*I am humbled by the gift!*
Let neglect break—*I am awakened to her worth!*
Let unity rise—*I am strengthened by divine partnership!*

I cry this over my children:
You are not called to chase riches—*you are called to*

recognize treasure!
You are not led by impulse—*you are led by discernment!*
You are not alone—*you are equipped with heaven's provision!*

So I rise and declare:
We honor what God gives.
We protect what God joins.
We build what God blesses.

We are the covenant keepers—
Wise in partnership,
Rich in purpose,
Unshaken in unity!

House and wealth are inherited from fathers, but a prudent wife is from the Lord. — Proverbs 19:14 (ESV)

BATTLE CRY 

I Love with Strength—I Respect with Honor—We Build with Unity!

> This is a **Battle Cry** of mutual honor, covenant strength, and love that reflects heaven's design–a cry that calls husbands to cherish, wives to respect, and both to build a legacy of unity and power. This isn't about hierarchy–it's about harmony, sacrificial love, and respect that fuels strength. It's the anthem of warriors who fight for each other, not against each other.

I do not love passively—*I love as I love myself!*
I do not lead with pride—*I lead with humility and care!*
I do not follow with fear—*I respect with fierce honor!*

I declare

Love is my weapon—*it heals, it covers, it empowers!*
Respect is my shield—*it protects, it uplifts, it strengthens!*
Unity is our legacy—*we fight together, not apart!*

This is our cry:
I love with strength—I respect with honor—we build with unity!
I do not neglect—I nurture!
I do not dishonor—I uplift!

Let selfishness fall—*we are one in purpose!*
Let division break—*we are fused by covenant!*
Let pride die—*we are anchored in love and respect!*

I cry this over my children:
You are not called to compete—*you are called to complete!*

**You are not called to dominate—*you are called to honor!*
You are not called to isolate—*you are called to unite in
love!***

So we rise and declare:
We love with intention.
We respect with fire.
We build with grace.
We reflect heaven's design.

We are the covenant builders—
Fierce in love,
Faithful in honor,
Unshaken in unity!

However, let each one of you love his wife as himself, and let
the wife see that she respects her husband.
— Ephesians 5:33 (ESV)

BATTLE CRY 

We Walk in Honor—We Lead with Love—We Build with Grace!

This is a **Battle Cry** of mutual honor, covenant strength, and Spirit-led partnership. A cry that calls both husband and wife to walk in divine order, serve with humility, and love with fierce gentleness. This is not about control, it's about *alignment, sacrificial leadership, and respect that reflects heaven's heart.*

I do not lead with harshness—*I lead with humility and strength!*
I do not follow in fear—*I submit with faith and honor!*
I do not fight for control—*I fight for covenant unity!*

I declare ⊢————
Submission is not silence—*it is sacred alignment!*
Love is not passive—*it is active sacrifice!*
Harshness has no place—*gentleness is our power!*

This is our cry:
We walk in honor—we lead with love—we build with grace!
I do not dominate—I cherish!
I do not resist—I respect!

Let pride fall—*we are clothed in humility!*
Let division break—*we are fused in purpose!*
Let harshness die—*we are gentle warriors of covenant love!*

I cry this over my children:
You are not called to control—*you are called to cherish!*

You are not called to rebellion—*you are called to respect!*
You are not called to strife—*you are called to build with grace!*

So we rise and declare:
We honor divine order.
We protect sacred unity.
We reflect the heart of Christ.

We are the covenant keepers—
Fierce in love,
Faithful in honor,
Unshaken in grace!

Wives, submit to your husbands, as is fitting in the Lord.
Husbands, love your wives, and do not be harsh with them.
— Colossians 3:18-19 (ESV)

I Love Fiercely—I Cover Deeply—I Heal What Sin Tried to Break!

This is a **Battle Cry** of relentless love, healing grace, and fierce forgiveness. A cry for warriors who love beyond offense, cover with compassion, and fight for unity through mercy. This is not soft love, it's earnest, enduring, and explosive in power. It's the anthem of those who know that **love is a weapon that heals what bitterness breaks.**

I do not love halfway—*I love with fire!*
I do not hold grudges—*I cover with grace!*
I do not expose—*I restore with mercy!*

I declare
Love is not weak—*it is warfare!*
Love is not passive—*it is active healing!*
Love is not optional—*it is my highest weapon!*

This is my cry:
I love fiercely—I cover deeply—I heal what sin tried to break!
I do not let offense win—I let love reign!
I do not keep score—I keep covenant!

Let bitterness fall—*I am clothed in compassion!*
Let division break—*I am fused by mercy!*
Let shame die—*I am covered by love that restores!*

I cry this over my children:
You are not called to punish—*you are called to cover!*
You are not called to resent—*you are called to restore!*

You are not called to fracture—*you are called to fight with love!*

So I rise and declare:
We love earnestly.
We forgive boldly.
We cover completely.
We heal fiercely.

We are the mercy warriors—
Unshaken by offense,
Unstoppable in love,
Unmatched in grace!

Above all, keep loving one another earnestly, since love covers a multitude of sins. — 1 Peter 4:8 (ESV)

BATTLE CRY 

I Guard the Gates—I Stand in Faith—I Fight with Courage—I Am Strong!

This is a **Battle Cry** of spiritual vigilance, unwavering conviction, and fierce **courage**. It is an anthem for those who refuse passivity, stand in bold faith, and rise with strength that doesn't back down. This is not gentle advice, it's a **command to the brave**, a rallying cry for **watchful warriors** and **unshaken** hearts.

I do not sleep while enemies scheme—*I stay alert in the Spirit!*
I do not waver in storms—*I stand firm in truth!*
I do not shrink back—*I move forward with lion-hearted courage!*
I do not faint—*I rise in supernatural strength!*

I declare

I am on guard—*no deception passes through!*
I am rooted—*no lie uproots my faith!*
I am courageous—*no fear shall lead me!*
I am strong—*no battle shall break me!*

This is my cry:
I guard the gates—I stand in faith—I fight with courage—I am strong!
I do not bow—I rise in battle!
I do not retreat—I press on in victory!

Let distraction fall—*I am focused on the mission!*
Let apathy break—*I am awakened in power!*
Let fear die—*I am filled with Spirit-born fire!*

I cry this over my children:
You are not fragile—you are *spiritual warriors!*
You are not passive—you are *bold and awake!*
You are not weak—you are *strengthened in faith!*

So I rise and declare:
We stay watchful.
We stand planted.
We move boldly.
We win fiercely.

We are the awakened—
Guardians of truth,
Champions of courage,
Unshaken in strength!

Be on your guard; stand firm in the faith; be courageous; be strong. — 1 Corinthians 16:13 (ESV)

BATTLE CRIES

For
Your Children

BATTLE CRY 

Fearless, Powerful, Loved, and Sound

This is the **Battle Cry** of a parent who refuses to let fear define their children. It's a bold declaration that *they are equipped by heaven with strength, love, and clarity, and they will rise with unshakable identity and divine authority.*

You were not given fear—*you were given fire!*
You were not born to tremble—*you were born to triumph!*
You do not carry panic—*you carry power, love, and a sound mind!*

Fear is not your inheritance—*faith is!*
Confusion is not your portion—*clarity is!*
Weakness is not your identity—*you are clothed in power and love!*

I declare over you
You will not shrink—*you will stand strong!*
You will not lash out—*you will love boldly!*
You will not spiral—*you will think clearly and walk wisely!*

Power is your posture.
Love is your language.
A sound mind is your shield—*and you wear it with confidence!*

So I cry out with holy fire and fierce protection:
My children are not ruled by fear—they are filled with power!
They are not tossed by emotion—they are anchored in love!
They are not lost in confusion—they walk with a sound mind!

Let fear knock—I answer with fire.
Let anxiety whisper—I respond with authority.
Let chaos press in—I declare: *"My children are fearless and fortified!"*

This is my battle cry for you—
You are not fragile, you are fierce.
You are not scattered, you are sound.
You are not afraid, you are anointed!
God has not given you fear—He has given you power, love, and a sound mind. So rise, my children, and walk in what heaven has placed within you!

God hath not given us the spirit of fear; but of power, and of love, and of a sound mind. — 2 Timothy 1:7 (KJV)

Battle Cry for My Children: Minds Set Like Steel—Hearts Fixed on Glory!

This is the **Battle Cry** of a parent who declares mental clarity, spiritual focus, and emotional strength over their children. It's a call to rise above distraction and darkness, and to fix their thoughts on the light of truth, beauty, and excellence.

You were not made to dwell in darkness—*you were made to fix your thoughts on light!*
You were not built for confusion—*you were built for clarity and truth!*
You do not follow the noise—*you follow what is noble, pure, and praiseworthy!*

Your mind is a battlefield—*but you are armed with truth!*
Your thoughts are sacred ground—*and I declare them filled with what is excellent!*
Your focus is your fire—*and I call it fixed on what is worthy of praise!*

I declare over you
You will not be swayed by lies—*you will stand in what is true!*
You will not be pulled by impurity—*you will rise in what is pure!*
You will not be distracted by chaos—*you will think on what is lovely and admirable!*

Truth is your compass.
Honor is your lens.

Excellence is your standard—and praise is your posture!

So I cry out with fierce conviction and holy fire:
My children will not be ruled by fear—they will be led by truth!
They will not be shaped by culture—they will be formed by what is right!
They will not be consumed by negativity—they will meditate on what is excellent!

Let the world flood their minds—*I declare: Their thoughts are fortified!*
Let lies try to creep in—I proclaim: *Their minds are guarded by truth!*
Let impurity knock—I roar: *Their focus is fixed on what is pure and praiseworthy!*

This is my battle cry for you—
You are not confused, you are clear.
You are not scattered, you are steady.
You are not lost in thought—you are locked onto what is true, honorable, and excellent!
Fix your thoughts, my children—and rise with minds set like steel and hearts full of praise!

And now, dear brothers and sisters, one final thing. Fix your thoughts on what is true, and honorable, and right, and pure, and lovely, and admirable. Think about things that are excellent and worthy of praise. — Philippians 4:8 (NKJV)

BATTLE CRY 

Fearless in Prayer, Grateful in Power!

This is the **Battle Cry** of a parent who equips their children with the weapons of prayer and gratitude. It's a declaration that anxiety has no authority, and that **peace flows from trust in a faithful God.**

You were not made to worry—*you were made to worship!*
You were not built for fear—*you were born for faith!*
You do not carry the weight alone—*you cast it into the hands of God!*

When anxiety attacks—*you answer with prayer!*
When needs arise—*you speak boldly to your Father!*
When the battle rages—*you fight with thanksgiving and trust!*

I declare over you
You will not be crushed by worry—*you will rise in peace!*
You will not be silenced by fear—*you will pray with power!*
You will not forget His goodness—*you will thank Him with fire in your heart!*

Prayer is your weapon.
Gratitude is your shield.
Trust is your stance—*and peace is your portion!*

So I cry out with fierce love and holy confidence:
My children will not worry—they will worship!

They will not panic—they will pray!
They will not forget—they will give thanks and walk in peace!

Let anxiety whisper—I answer with intercession.
Let fear rise—I respond with faith.
Let pressure press in—I declare: *"My children are anchored in prayer and overflowing with praise!"*

This is my battle cry for you—
You are not anxious, you are armored in peace.
You are not helpless, you are heard by heaven.
You are not overwhelmed, you are overflowing with gratitude!
So pray about everything, thank Him for all He's done—and walk boldly into every day!

Don't worry about anything; instead, pray about everything. Tell God what you need, and thank him for all he has done.
— Philippians 4:6 (NLT)

God Is for You—So Rise, Unshaken!

This is the **Battle Cry** of a parent who declares divine backing over their children. It's a fearless proclamation that no opposition can stand, no threat can prevail, and no voice can silence what God has ordained.

What shall we say to fear? *God is for you!*
What shall we say to doubt? *God is for you!*
What shall we say to every enemy, every lie, every storm?
God is for you—and nothing can stand against you!

You are not alone—*Heaven fights beside you!*
You are not weak—*the Almighty strengthens you!*
You are not vulnerable—*you are backed by the power of God Himself!*

I declare over you
You will not bow to fear—*you will rise in faith!*
You will not shrink from battle—*you will stand in boldness!*
You will not be defeated—*you will walk in victory!*

God is your defender.
God is your shield.
God is your banner—*and He goes before you!*

So I cry out with holy fire and unwavering confidence:
My children are not victims—they are victors!

They are not alone—they are aligned with heaven!
They are not outnumbered—they are overshadowed by
divine strength!

Let the world rise against them—I declare: *God is for them!*
Let trials press in—I proclaim: *God surrounds them!*
Let voices speak against them—I roar: *God has the final
word!*

This is my battle cry for you—
You are not forsaken, you are fiercely defended.
You are not fragile, you are fortified by faith.
You are not outmatched, you are empowered by the One
who reigns!
If God is for you—who can ever be against you?

What shall we say about such wonderful things as these? If
God is for us, who can ever be against us.
— Romans 8:31 (NLT)

BATTLE CRY

You Rise in Mercy—You Stand in Faithfulness!

> This is the **Battle Cry** of a parent who declares that every morning their children wake up wrapped in mercy, covered in love, and empowered by the unshakable faithfulness of God.

You are not defined by yesterday—*His mercies are new today!*
You are not bound by failure—*His faithful love never ends!*
You are not alone—*you rise in the presence of a faithful God!*

His love does not run dry—*it floods your life with hope!*
His mercy does not expire—*it renews your strength each morning!*
His faithfulness does not falter—*it anchors your soul through every storm!*

I declare over you
You will not be crushed—*you are carried by compassion!*
You will not be consumed—*you are covered by covenant!*
You will not be forgotten—*you are favored by faithfulness!*

Each sunrise brings fresh mercy.
Each breath is proof of His love.
Each step is guided by His unwavering grace.

So I cry out with fierce devotion and holy confidence:
My children rise in mercy—they walk in the strength of His love!

They are not stuck—they are renewed daily!
They are not weak—they are warriors of grace!

Let shame speak—I silence it with mercy.
Let fear creep—I crush it with faithfulness.
Let weariness weigh down—I lift them with love that
never ends!

This is my battle cry for you— ⚔
You are not forgotten, you are fiercely loved.
You are not weary, you are freshly strengthened.
You are not broken, you are being rebuilt every morning!
Great is His faithfulness—so rise, my children, and walk
in mercy's power!

The faithful love of the Lord never ends! His mercies never cease. Great is his faithfulness; his mercies begin afresh each morning. — Lamentations 3:22-23 (NLT)

BATTLE CRY

You Are Masterpieces—Made to Move Mountains!

> This is the **Battle Cry** of a parent who sees divine design in every detail of their children's lives. It's a declaration of identity, purpose, and power, crafted by heaven, called to goodness, and destined for impact.

You are not ordinary—*you are God's masterpiece!*
You are not random—*you are crafted with eternal intention!*
You are not forgotten—*you are created anew in Christ Jesus!*

You were formed by the Artist of heaven—*with precision, with purpose, with power!*
You were made for good works—*not someday, but now!*
You were chosen to walk in destiny—*not drift in doubt!*

I declare over you
You will not shrink—you will *shine!*
You will not wander—you will *walk boldly in purpose!*
You will not be silenced—you will *speak life and truth!*

Your identity is sealed in Christ.
Your future is filled with divine assignments.
Your steps are ordered by the One who planned them long ago.

So I cry out with fierce love and unwavering faith:
You are masterpieces—marked by heaven, made for greatness!

You are not accidents—you are answers to the world's need!
You are not weak—you are warriors of goodness!

Let insecurity whisper—I answer with identity.
Let confusion rise—I respond with clarity.
Let the world question—I declare: "My children are
handcrafted by God and launched into purpose!"

This is my battle cry for you—
You are not average, you are anointed.
You are not overlooked, you are ordained.
You are not unfinished—you are unfolding the
masterpiece of heaven!
Created anew in Christ Jesus—go and do the good things
He planned for you!

We are God's masterpiece. He has created us anew in Christ
Jesus, so we can do the good things he planned for us long
ago. — Ephesians 2:10 (NLT)

Covered by Wings, Armored by Promise!

This is the **Battle Cry** of a parent who fiercely declares divine protection, refuge, and rest over their children. It's a shield of faith, a roar of trust, and a mantle of mercy wrapped in the wings of the Almighty.

My children do not walk alone—they dwell in the shelter
of the Most High!
They do not sleep in fear—they rest in the shadow of the
Almighty!
They do not face danger uncovered—they are wrapped in
His wings!

He alone is their refuge—not the world, not my strength,
but the Lord!
He alone is their safety—not luck, not chance, but
covenant protection!
He alone is their God—and I trust Him with their every
breath!

Every trap will fail—because He rescues them!
Every disease will flee—because He shields them!
Every fear will fall—because His promises are their armor!

His feathers are their fortress.
His wings are their wall.
His truth is their shield—*and I declare it over them daily!*

So I cry out with holy fire and parental faith:
My children are covered, not crushed!
They are sheltered, not shaken!
They are armored in promise, not exposed to peril!

Let the enemy plot—I stand between.
Let the storm rage—I raise my voice.
Let fear whisper—I roar back with trust!

This is my battle cry for you—
You are not vulnerable, you are victorious.
You are not fragile, you are fortified.
You are not alone, you are anchored in the Almighty!
You dwell in His shelter, rest in His shadow, and rise in
His promises!

Those who live in the shelter of the Most High will find
rest in the shadow of the Almighty. This I declare about the
Lord: He alone is my refuge, my place of safety; he is my
God, and I trust him. For he will rescue you from every trap
and protect you from deadly disease. He will cover you with
his feathers. He will shelter you with his wings. His faithful
promises are your armor and protection.
— Psalm 91:1-4 (NLT)

Mercy Is Moving—You Were Made for Redemption!

This is the **Battle Cry** of a parent who sees divine patience not as delay, but as destiny. It's a fierce proclamation that their children are part of heaven's redemptive plan, called to rise in righteousness and walk in the fullness of God's promise.

My children are not forgotten—they are being formed in mercy's timing!
The promise is not slow—it is sacred, unfolding with precision!
The waiting is not wasted—it is woven with purpose for your sake!

The Lord is patient—*because He loves you deeply!*
He holds back judgment—*because He longs for your repentance!*
He delays destruction—*because He desires your destiny!*

You were not born for ruin—*you were born for redemption!*
You were not made to wander—*you were made to return!*
You were not created to perish—*you were called to rise in repentance!*

His patience is your protection.
His kindness is your invitation.
His promise is your pathway—*and I will fight for you to walk it!*

So I cry out with holy fire:
My children are not lost—they are loved!
They are not delayed—they are being drawn!
They are not destroyed—they are destined to repent and reign!

Let the enemy whisper lies—I answer with truth.
Let the world rush—I wait with purpose.
Let fear rise—I respond with faith.

This is my battle cry for you—
You are not forgotten, you are being pursued.
You are not forsaken, you are being formed.
You are not doomed, you are destined for divine turnaround!
The Lord is patient for your sake—and I will stand in the gap until you rise!

The Lord isn't really being slow about his promise, as some people think. No, he is being patient for your sake. He does not want anyone to be destroyed but wants everyone to repent. — 2 Peter 3:9 (NLT)

You Are Marked by Promise, Destined for Glory!

This is the **Battle Cry** of a parent who sees **heaven's blueprint etched into their child's soul**. It's a declaration of fierce love, divine destiny, and unwavering hope.

You are not random—*you are written into God's plan!*
You are not overlooked—*you are seen by the Author of eternity!*
You are not fragile—*you are forged for a future filled with hope!*

The Lord has plans for you—*not disaster, but destiny!*
His thoughts toward you are good—*not vague, but victorious!*
Your future is not a question mark—*it's a promise sealed by heaven!*

I speak life over you—*not fear, but fire!*
I declare purpose in you—*not confusion, but clarity!*
I call forth greatness from you—*not delay, but divine acceleration!*

You are covered by covenant.
You are surrounded by grace.
You are launched by love—*and nothing can stop what God has started!*

So I cry out with boldness and blessing:
You are God's masterpiece—crafted for good, crowned
with hope!
You will rise—you will run—you will roar with purpose!
Your future is not fragile—it is fortified by the Father!

Let doubt whisper—I answer with destiny.
Let fear creep—I respond with fire.
Let the world question—I declare: *My child is chosen,
cherished, and called!*

This is my battle cry for you—
You are not a maybe, you are a miracle.
You are not a shadow, you are a spark.
You are not a statistic, you are a story of divine hope!
I know the plans He has for you—and I will fight for
every promise to come alive!

"I know the plans I have for you," says the Lord. "They are plans for good and not for disaster, to give you a future and a hope." — Jeremiah 29:11 (NLT)

I Train Them to Triumph—Their Path Is Lit with Purpose!

This is the **Battle Cry** of a legacy-minded warrior who knows that every word, every prayer, every moment of guidance is a seed of destiny. It's a declaration that your children are being shaped for victory, and that the path they walk will echo into eternity.

I do not guess their future—*I guide it with truth!*
I do not hope they'll find the way—*I start them on it with fire!*
I do not fear the world's pull—*I trust the power of God's path!*

I train them in righteousness—*not religion, but relationship!*
I speak identity into their spirit—*not confusion, but clarity!*
I plant purpose in their hearts—*not passivity, but power!*

I declare over them
They will not drift—*they will drive forward in destiny!*
They will not forget—*they will flourish in the way of the Lord!*
They will not turn away—*they will turn the world upside down with truth!*

Their path is marked by heaven.
Their steps are ordered by God.
Their future is sealed with promise—*and I will not stop declaring it!*

So I cry out with generational fire:
I train them to triumph—I start them strong, and they
will finish fierce!
They will not be lost—they are led by light!
They will not be shaken—they are rooted in truth!

Let culture try to sway them—I declare: *Their foundation
is firm!*
Let lies try to lure them—I proclaim: *Their compass is
Christ!*
Let time pass—I roar: *They will not turn from the way—
they will rise in it!*

This is my battle cry—
I do not just raise children—I raise warriors.
I do not just teach lessons—I launch legacies.
I do not just hope for the best—I declare the path, and
they will walk it with fire!
Start them strong, and they will finish faithful!

"Start children off on the way they should go, and even when
they are old they will not turn from it."
— Proverbs 22:6 (NIV)

I Build, Not Break—I Train with Truth, Not Tyranny!

This **Battle Cry** is for fathers and spiritual leaders who reject harshness and choose holy instruction. It's a declaration of intentional parenting, where strength is tempered by grace, and authority is wielded to uplift, not oppress.

I do not provoke—*I protect!*
I do not crush—*I cultivate!*
I do not demand—*I disciple!*

I am not a tyrant—I am a trainer.
I am not a storm—I am a shelter.
I am not a wound—I am a wellspring of wisdom.

I declare
My words will not bruise—they will *build!*
My discipline will not destroy—it will *develop!*
My instruction will not confuse—it will *clarify!*

I raise warriors—not worriers.
I speak life—not labels.
I lead with love—not fear.

I cry out:
I will not exasperate—I will elevate!
I train with truth—I instruct with integrity!
My children will rise—not recoil!

Let the world model rage—I choose *righteousness!*
Let culture teach control—I choose *compassion!*
Let pride provoke—I choose *purpose!*

This is my battle cry—
I do not parent by pressure—I parent by promise.
I do not lead with fists—I lead with faith.
I do not command obedience—I cultivate understanding.
I bring them up in the Lord—not down in frustration.
I am a father forged by grace—and my children will
flourish in it!

Fathers, do not exasperate your children; instead, bring them up in the training and instruction of the Lord.
— Ephesians 6:4 (NIV)

I Impress the Word—I Ignite Legacy!

This is the **Battle Cry** of a parent who refuses to let truth fade with time. It's a declaration of generational fire, where the Word of God is not just taught, but engraved into the hearts of their children through daily rhythm, relentless love, and intentional discipleship.

I do not whisper truth—*I impress it with fire!*
I do not delegate discipleship—*I own it with passion!*
I do not wait for the perfect moment—
I make every moment sacred!

The Word is on my heart—*and I press it into theirs!*
I speak it when we sit—*because home is holy ground!*
I speak it when we walk—
because every step is a chance to shape destiny!
I speak it when we lie down—*because rest is wrapped in revelation!*
I speak it when we rise—*because mornings are made for mission!*

I declare
My children will not be starved of truth—
they will feast on it daily!
They will not be shaped by culture—
they will be carved by covenant!
They will not forget the Word—
they will carry it like fire in their bones!

I am a messenger of legacy.
I am a teacher of truth.
I am a warrior of the Word—*and my children are my mission!*

So I cry out with generational fire:
I impress the Word—I ignite legacy!
I speak truth in every season, every setting, every step!
My children will rise with scripture in their soul and strength in their spirit!

Let distraction try to steal—I answer with devotion.
Let silence try to settle—I respond with scripture.
Let forgetfulness creep in—I roar:
"The Word is written on our hearts!"

This is my battle cry—
I do not just raise children—I raise carriers of covenant.
I do not just teach—I transform.
I do not just hope they remember—I make sure they never forget.
The Word is our rhythm, our roar, our legacy—and I will impress it until they rise in it!

These commandments that I give you today are to be on your hearts. Impress them on your children. Talk about them when you sit at home and when you walk along the road, when you lie down and when you get up.
— Deuteronomy 6:6-7(NIV)

BATTLE CRIES

For
Friendships

I Love at All Times—I Stand in Adversity—I Fight Beside My Friend!

> This is a powerful foundation for a **Battle Cry** that honors loyalty, love, and fierce friendship–the kind that stands through storms, lifts in weakness, and fights beside you in adversity. It's a declaration for those who don't just walk with you in success, but war with you in struggle.

I do not flee when the storm hits—*I stand firmer!*
I do not love by convenience—*I love by covenant!*
I do not watch from a distance—*I step into the fire with you!*

I declare
I am a friend forged in faith.
I am a brother born for battle.
I am a warrior of loyalty and love.

This is my cry:
**I love at all times—I stand in adversity—
I fight beside my friend!
I do not abandon—I anchor!
I do not retreat—I reinforce!**

Let betrayal fall—*I am faithful to the end!*
Let isolation break—*I am present in the pain!*
Let fear flee—*I am fierce in friendship!*

I cry this over my relationships, my circle, my calling:

I am not just a companion—I am a covenant keeper!
I am not just a friend—I am a fortress in adversity!
I am not just loyal—I am love in motion!

So I rise and declare:
I love without limits.
I stand without wavering.
I fight without fear.

I reflect heaven's heart.
I am the faithful—
Friend of fire,
Brother and Sisters in battle,
Unshaken in love!

A friend loves at all times, and a brother is born for a time of adversity. — Proverbs 17:17 (NIV)

Sharpened in Spirit, United in Strength

This is a spiritually resonant, emotionally rich Battle Cry built around crafted to echo the power of friendship as divine sharpening, legacy-building, and soul-forging:

"As iron sharpens iron, so one person sharpens another."
We are not solitary blades—we are forged in fellowship.
In the sacred tension of truth and love, we are refined.
In the heat of challenge and grace, we are shaped.
Friendship is not comfort—it is the forge of heaven.

We do not fear friction.
We welcome the strike of honesty, the flame of encouragement, the edge of accountability.
For in the presence of a true friend, dullness is driven out, purpose is revealed, and destiny is ignited.

We declare
I am not sharpened by silence—I am honed by truth.
I am not strengthened by flattery—I am refined by love that dares to correct.
I am not called to isolation—I am built for covenant connection.

When I grow weary, my brother lifts me.
When I lose sight, my sister speaks light.
When I falter, my friend becomes my fortress.

Together, we rise.
So we cry out:
Sharpen me, Lord, through those You've placed beside me.
Make me a blade of legacy—cutting through fear, forging
hope, and defending truth.
Let our friendship be a forge of heaven—where sparks fly,
edges gleam, and warriors rise.

As iron sharpens iron, so one person sharpens another.
— Proverbs 27:17 (NIV)

Face to Face, Heart to Heart

This is a spiritually grounded, emotionally resonant **Battle Cry** that emphasizes the sacred responsibility of resolving conflict with integrity, humility, and directness–especially within the bonds of friendship.

We are warriors of truth, not whisperers of offense.
We do not scatter wounds—we seek healing at the source.
In friendship, we fight for restoration, not reputation.

If conflict arises, we do not run to the crowd.
We do not trade trust for gossip, nor loyalty for leverage.
We go directly—to the one who matters most.
Because friendship is a covenant, not a courtroom.

We declare

Let my words be seasoned with grace, not sharpened for
accusation.
Let my heart be bold enough to confront, humble enough
to listen.
Let my loyalty be proven in private, not paraded in public.

I will not betray confidence for the sake of being right.
I will not invite shame by airing wounds before strangers.
I will not let the charge against me stand—when
reconciliation is within reach.

Instead, I rise:
To speak truth in love.

To restore what was broken.
To protect what was sacred.

So I cry out:
Lord, make me a keeper of trust, a restorer of peace,
A friend who fights for unity, not division.
Let my battle be for healing—not for victory over my
brother.

If you take your neighbor to court, do not betray another's confidence, the one who hears it may shame you and the charge against you will stand. — Proverbs 25:9-10 (NIV)

Bound in Light, Unshaken by Darkness

This is a spiritually discerning **Battle Cry** that honors the sacred nature of godly friendship and is crafted to affirm the importance of walking in unity with those who share the light, while calling believers to guard their hearts and align their relationships with righteousness.

We are not bound by convenience—
we are yoked by covenant.
We do not walk in step with shadows—*we stride in the brilliance of truth.*
Our friendships are not casual—*they are consecrated.*

We declare
I will not link arms with what dims my fire.
I will not tether my soul to what denies the Spirit.
I will not trade eternal purpose for temporary peace.

For friendship is not merely connection—it is alignment.
It is the joining of hearts, the blending of paths, the forging of legacy.
And I will walk only with those who sharpen my spirit, not dull my conviction.

I rise with those who carry light.
I stand beside those who speak truth.
I fight alongside those who know the name of the Lord.

So I cry out:
Let my friendships be holy ground.
Let my alliances reflect heaven's design.
Let me be yoked only to those who run toward
righteousness,
That together, we may plow the fields of purpose,
Break the ground of legacy,
And reap the harvest of eternal glory.

Do not be yoked together with unbelievers. For what do righteousness and wickedness have in common? Or what fellowship can light have with darkness?
— 2 Corinthians 6:14 (NIV)

BATTLE CRY

Covenant Companions

We do not stand alone. We do not fall apart.
We are a threefold cord—woven by God, strengthened by
love, sealed in truth.
We are not easily broken. We are not easily shaken.
We rise together. We fight together. We win together.

When one grows weary, the other becomes strength.
When one is wounded, the other becomes healing.
We are not fragile—we are forged in faith.

We speak life over one another.
We declare identity, purpose, and victory.
Our words are weapons. Our unity is armor.

Our bond is a fortress. Our friendship is a banner.
We are covenant companions—chosen, called, connected.
We are a legacy of power, a testimony of grace.

We will not be broken.
We will not be silenced.
We are warriors of love, defenders of destiny.

Together, we stand.
Together, we overcome.
Together, we roar.

And though a man might prevail against one who is alone, two will withstand him—a threefold cord is not quickly broken. — Ecclesiastes 4:12 (ESV)

Fierce Friendship

> This is a **Battle Cry for Friendships**, shaped to echo through generations. It's designed to be spoken aloud, declared in unity, or passed on as a legacy of love that fights, heals, and endures.

We do not love lightly. We love like warriors.
Love is our weapon—patient in the fire, kind in the storm.
We do not envy. We do not boast.
We rise in humility, not arrogance.
We walk in honor, not offense.

We do not insist on our own way.
We lay down pride and pick up grace.
We are not irritable. We are not resentful.
We forgive quickly. We protect fiercely.

We do not rejoice in wrongdoing.
We rejoice in truth, even when it costs us.
We bear all things—together.
We believe all things—together.
We hope all things—together.
We endure all things—together.

This is friendship forged in fire.
This is love that does not fail.
We are covenant companions.
We are defenders of each other's hearts.
We are builders of legacy, carriers of truth.

We love like warriors.

And we will not be broken.

Love is patient and kind; love does not envy or boast; it is not arrogant or rude. It does not insist on its own way; it is not irritable or resentful; it does not rejoice at wrongdoing, but rejoices with the truth. Love bears all things, believes all things, hopes all things, endures all things.
— 1 Corinthians 13:4-7 (ESV)

Sacrificial Friendship

This is a **Battle Cry of Sacrificial Friendship**, shaped to honor the kind of love that defends, endures, and lays down everything for another. It's crafted to be spoken aloud with conviction–whether in ministry, legacy moments, or personal prayer.

We do not love for comfort. We love to the death.
Greater love has no one than this—
That we would lay down our lives for our friends.
Not just in death, but in daily surrender.
We lay down pride. We lay down fear.
We lay down our own way to lift another.

We are not fair-weather companions.
We are covenant keepers.
We do not run when the battle rages.
We stand. We shield. We sacrifice.

Our friendship is not fragile.
It is forged in fire, sealed in truth, and sustained by grace.
We carry each other's burdens.
We fight for each other's healing.
We speak life when silence would be easier.

We are defenders of destiny.
We are protectors of purpose.
We are warriors of love.

This is the friendship that lays down its life.
This is the love that cannot be shaken.
This is the bond that builds legacy.

We do not retreat.
We do not abandon.
We love like Christ.

And we will not be broken.

Greater love has no one than this, that someone lay down his life for his friends. — John 15:13 (ESV)

BATTLE CRY

Uplifting Friendship

We do not tear down. We build. We do not abandon. We strengthen.
We are not casual companions—we are kingdom allies.
We speak life into weary souls.
We lift arms that are tired from battle.
We call out greatness when others forget who they are.

We do not compete—we complete.
We do not compare—we champion.
We do not criticize—we construct.

We are builders of courage.
We are architects of hope.
We are defenders of destiny.

We encourage with fire.
We affirm with truth.
We build with love.

Our words are not empty—they are weapons.
Our presence is not passive—it is power.
Our friendship is not fragile—it is forged in heaven.

We rise together.
We roar together.
We build one another up—brick by brick, word by word,
prayer by prayer.

We are covenant companions.
We are fierce encouragers.
We are legacy builders.

And we will not be broken.

Therefore encourage one another and build one another up, just as you are doing. — 1 Thessalonians 5:11 (ESV)

Christ-like Friendship

This is a **Battle Cry of Christlike Friendship**, shaped to echo with divine authority, legacy, and fierce love. It's designed to be declared aloud—whether in ministry, devotion, or moments of generational blessing.

We do not love by feeling. We love by command. We love by covenant.
A new commandment has been given—not a suggestion,
not a sentiment.
We are commanded to love one another—
Not as the world loves, but as Christ loves.

We love with sacrifice.
We love with truth.
We love with fire.

We lay down pride.
We lay down offense.
We lay down our lives.

We do not abandon.
We do not betray.
We do not forget.

We love with loyalty.
We love with legacy.
We love with the power of heaven behind us.

This is not fragile friendship.
This is fierce, holy alliance.
This is love that defends, restores, and endures.

We are covenant companions.
We are Christlike friends.
We are warriors of love.

And we will not be broken.

A new commandment I give to you, that you love one another: just as I have loved you, you also are to love one another. — John 13:34 (ESV)

Peaceful Friendship

This is a **Battle Cry of Peaceful Friendship**, shaped to roar with humility, gentleness, and fierce commitment to unity. It's crafted to be spoken aloud with conviction–perfect for ministry, legacy moments, or declarations over relationships that are meant to endure.

We do not fight for dominance. We fight for unity.
We walk in humility—
not weakness, but strength under control.
We speak with gentleness—
not silence, but power wrapped in grace.
We wait with patience—not passivity, but fierce endurance.

We bear with one another in love—
Not because it's easy, but because it's holy.
Not because we agree on everything,
But because we are bound by something greater.

We make every effort—every prayer, every word, every
sacrifice—
To keep the unity of the Spirit.
We do not tear down what heaven has built.
We do not abandon what God has joined.

Our bond is not casual—it is covenant.
Our peace is not fragile—it is forged in faith.
Our friendship is not temporary—it is legacy.

We are peacemakers.
We are burden-bearers.
We are builders of unity.

We fight for each other.
We fight beside each other.
We fight to remain one.

And we will never be broken.

With all humility and gentleness, with patience, bearing with one another in love. Make every effort to keep the unity of the Spirit through the bond of peace. — Ephesians 4:2 (ESV)

BATTLE CRY 

Discerning Friendship

This is a **Battle Cry of Discerning Friendship** and is built for warriors who choose their companions with purpose, knowing that legacy depends on alignment.

We do not walk blindly. We walk with fire and wisdom.
We walk with the wise—
Because wisdom is contagious, and we are carriers of truth.
We walk with those who fear God,
Because reverence builds resilience.

We do not link arms with fools.
We do not entertain chaos.
We do not suffer harm for the sake of comfort.

We choose our circle like we choose our weapons—
Sharpened, tested, and ready for battle.
We surround ourselves with those who speak life,
Who build legacy,
Who war in prayer and walk in peace.

We are not easily swayed.
We are not easily deceived.
We are not easily broken.

We walk with the wise—
And we become wise.
We walk with the faithful—
And we become fierce.

This is friendship with fire.
This is alliance with purpose.
This is legacy forged in discernment.

We are covenant companions.
We are guardians of influence.
We are warriors of wisdom.

And we will never be broken.

Whoever walks with the wise becomes wise, but the companion of fools will suffer harm. — Proverbs 13:20 (NIV)

BATTLE CRY 

Layered Friendship

We do not drift into greatness. We climb. We build. We war for it.
We begin with faith—
Not just belief, but bold trust that anchors us in every
storm.
We add virtue—
Because character is our armor, and integrity our sword.

We pursue knowledge—
Not to impress, but to understand, to sharpen, to protect.
We walk in self-control—
Because restraint is strength, and friendship without
boundaries breaks.

We stand in steadfastness—
Because loyalty is louder than words and stronger than
time.
We rise in godliness—
Because our bond reflects heaven, not the world.

We carry brotherly affection—
Because we are not just allies—we are family.
And we crown it all with love—
Fierce, sacrificial, enduring love that never fails.

This is friendship that climbs.
This is relationship that refines.
This is legacy that lasts.

We do not settle.
We do not fracture.
We do not forget the climb.

We build with faith.
We war with virtue.
We finish with love.

And we will not be broken.

For this very reason, make every effort to supplement your faith with virtue, and virtue with knowledge, and knowledge with self-control, and self-control with steadfastness, and steadfastness with godliness, and godliness with brotherly affection, and brotherly affection with love.
— 2 Peter 1:5-7 (NIV)

BATTLE CRIES

For
Overcoming Temptation

BATTLE CRY
of the Unshaken

This **Battle Cry** is one that speaks not only to the moment of temptation, but to endurance, covenant strength, and divine escape.

We do not tremble at temptation.
We do not bow to pressure.
We are not prey to the schemes of darkness—
We are heirs of endurance, warriors of the Way maker.

No temptation has overtaken us
Except what is common to mankind.
But we are not bound by what is common—
We are marked by covenant, sealed by grace,
And armed with the promises of a faithful God.

God is faithful.
Not distant. Not delayed. Not distracted.
He is present in the pressure,
Precise in the provision,
And powerful in the path He carves through the chaos.

He will not let us be tempted beyond what we can bear.
We are not fragile.
We are fortified.
We are forged in the fire of His Word.

When temptation rises like a flood,
We do not drown.
We do not drift.
We do not despair.
We look for the way out—because He provides it.

A door in the wall.
A light in the tunnel.
A whisper in the storm.

We endure—not by our strength,
But by His Spirit.
We escape—not by our cleverness,
But by His covenant.

We are not defined by the trial.
We are defined by the triumph.
We are not shaped by the pressure.
We are shaped by the promise.

SO WE DECLARE:
We will not be overtaken.
We will not be broken.
We will not be silenced.

We are the unshaken.
We are the enduring.
We are the ones who walk through fire
And come out radiant.

Temptation is not our tomb.
It is the threshold of testimony.

No temptation has overtaken you except what is common to mankind. And God is faithful; he will not let you be tempted beyond what you can bear. But when you are tempted, he will also provide a way out so that you can endure it.
— 1 Corinthians 10:13 (NIV)

BATTLE CRY
of the Faithful Shield

This **Battle Cry** is to **declare divine strength and protection** in the face of spiritual warfare, temptation, and any battle.

We do not stand alone. We are held, strengthened, and shielded by the Faithful One.

The Lord is faithful.

Not once. Not sometimes.

Always.

In the silence, in the storm, in the shadow—He is there.

He does not forget. He does not fail. He does not flinch.

He strengthens us.

When our knees buckle, He braces us.

When our hearts tremble, He steadies us.

When our courage wanes, He breathes fire into our bones.

We are not weaklings in the fight.

We are warriors wrapped in divine resolve.

We are sons and daughters of the Strong Tower.

He protects us from the evil one.

Not with fragile walls, but with unbreakable covenant.

Not with fleeting comfort, but with eternal covering.

The enemy may roar,

But we do not retreat.

The darkness may press,

But we do not fold.

We are shielded by the Word.
We are guarded by the Spirit.
We are surrounded by the faithfulness of God.

SO WE RISE AND DECLARE:
I am not alone. I am not exposed. I am not defeated.
The Lord is my strength. The Lord is my shield.
The Lord is faithful—and I am fearless.

We walk forward—not in fear, but in fire.
We stand firm—not in pride, but in promise.
We fight—not for victory, but from it.

We are the protected.
We are the empowered.
We are the living proof of His faithfulness.

But the Lord is faithful, and he will strengthen you and protect you from the evil one. — 2 Thessalonians 3:3 (NIV)

BATTLE CRY
of the Unforsaken

This is a Battle Cry to **stir courage, covenant loyalty, and spiritual defiance** in the face of fear.

We do not flinch. We do not flee. We are not alone—and we will not be moved.

Be strong. Be courageous.
This is not a suggestion.
It is a summons.
A call to rise, to roar, to resist.

We do not tremble before giants.
We do not cower before threats.
We do not shrink in the shadow of fear.

For the LORD our God goes with us.
Not behind. Not beside.
He goes before us—
A consuming fire, a mighty shield, a voice that splits the silence.

He does not abandon.
He does not forget.
He does not forsake.

We are not orphans in the battle.
We are covenant warriors.
We are flame-bearers.
We are sons and daughters of the Unshakable One.

SO WE DECLARE:
I will not be afraid.
I will not be terrified.
I will not be silenced by fear or swallowed by doubt.

The Lord goes with me—
Into the valley, onto the battlefield, through the storm.
He walks with me in fire.
He fights with me in silence.
He stands with me in victory.

I am not forsaken. I am not forgotten. I am not fragile.
I am fierce.
I am faithful.
I am fortified.
Let the enemy tremble.
Let the darkness scatter.

Let the heavens hear our cry:
We are the unafraid.
We are the unshaken.
We are the ones who rise—because He walks with us.

Be strong and courageous. Do not be afraid or terrified because
of them, for the LORD your God goes with you; he will never
leave you nor forsake you. — Deuteronomy 31:6 (NIV)

BATTLE CRY
of the Upheld: Fearless by His Hand

This is a covenant-rooted **Battle Cry**, that speaks **strength into the soul, fire into the spirit**, and unshakable trust into every battlefield moment.

We do not fear. We do not flinch. We do not fold beneath the weight
of war.
For He is with us.
Not distant. Not silent. Not delayed.
He is present in the pressure,
Thunder in the silence,
Fire in the stillness.

We are not dismayed.
Not by the size of the enemy,
Not by the chaos of the moment,
Not by the shadows that whisper lies.

He is our God.
Not just in name—but in covenant.
Not just in theory—but in power.
Not just in history—but in this very breath.

He strengthens us—
With might that does not waver,
With courage that does not crack,
With resolve that does not run.

He helps us—
Not as a distant observer,
But as a warrior beside us,
A Father before us,
A King within us.

He upholds us with His righteous right hand.
Not a trembling grip.
Not a temporary hold.
But an eternal grasp that does not let go.

SO WE RISE AND DECLARE:
I will not fear.
I will not be dismayed.
I will not be shaken.

I am upheld.
I am helped.
I am strengthened.

I am not prey—I am a pillar.
I am not broken—I am battle-born.
I am not alone—I am held by the hand that forged the stars.

Let the enemy rage.
Let the winds howl.
Let the darkness press.

We stand—
Fearless.
Faithful.
Upheld.

So do not fear, for I am with you; do not be dismayed, for I am your God. I will strengthen you and help you; I will uphold you with my righteous right hand.
— Isaiah 41:10 (NIV)

BATTLE CRY
of the Watchful and Wise

This is a **Battle Cry** to declare the power of divine discernment and understanding as weapons of protection, especially in the face of deception and spiritual warfare.

We do not charge blindly. We walk with eyes wide, hearts guarded, and spirits sharpened.
Discretion is our shield.
Not hesitation. Not fear.
But holy restraint—
The wisdom to wait, the clarity to see,
The courage to choose what others overlook.

Understanding is our armor.
Not mere knowledge, but divine insight.
It guards our steps,
It filters the noise,
It exposes the schemes of the enemy.

We do not fall for every voice.
We do not chase every fire.
We do not follow every crowd.

We are watchful. We are wise. We are warriors of discernment.

We listen for the whisper of the Spirit.
We see beyond the surface.
We walk paths lit by revelation, not impulse.

SO WE DECLARE:
I am not reckless. I am not deceived. I am not exposed.
I am protected by discretion.
I am guarded by understanding.
I am led by the wisdom of the Most High.

Let the enemy plot.
Let confusion rise.
Let deception swirl.

We stand—
Clear-eyed.
Spirit-led.
Unshaken.

We are the ones who see.
We are the ones who wait.
We are the ones who walk in wisdom and war in truth.

Discretion will protect you, and understanding will guard you. — Proverbs 2:11(NIV)

BATTLE CRY
of Wisdom's Watch

This is a **Battle Cry** to awaken reverence, spiritual discernment, and covenant protection.

We do not walk blind. We are guarded by wisdom, watched by understanding, and led by the voice of truth.
Do not forsake wisdom—
She is not fragile.
She is fierce.
She is the shield that does not crack,
The voice that does not lie,
The guardian who does not sleep.

We do not chase noise.
We do not follow impulse.
We do not trade truth for comfort.

We love wisdom—
And she watches over us.
Not passively, but fiercely.
Not distantly, but intimately.
She stands at the gates.
She walks the walls.
She whispers in the storm.

We are not reckless.
We are not deceived.
We are not exposed.

We are the ones who listen.
We are the ones who wait.
We are the ones who walk in light.

SO WE DECLARE:
I will not forsake wisdom.
I will not abandon truth.
I will not walk unguarded.

She protects me—
From the trap,
From the lie,
From the counterfeit crown.

She watches over me—
In the silence,
In the battle,
In the legacy I leave behind.

I am not alone. I am not unarmed. I am not unaware.
I am watched.
I am guarded.
I am wise.

Let the enemy scheme.
Let deception rise.
Let confusion swirl.
Spirit-led.
Unshaken.

We are the ones who love wisdom—
And she loves us back with fire in her eyes.

Do not forsake wisdom, and she will protect you; love her,
and she will watch over you. — Proverbs 4:6 (NIV)

BATTLE CRY
of the Sheltered and Singing

This **Battle Cry** is to stir joy in the midst of warfare, declare divine protection over those who love His name, and awaken a legacy of gladness that roars louder than fear.

*We do not hide in fear. We take refuge in glory. We rejoice
beneath the shield of His name.*
Let all who take refuge in the Lord be glad—
Not timid, not trembling, but triumphant.
We do not run to escape.
We run to be embraced.
We run to be covered by the wings of the Almighty.

We sing for joy—not after the battle, but in the middle of it.
Our praise is not passive.
It is a weapon.
It is a war cry.
It is the sound of victory before the victory is seen.

Spread Your protection over us, O Lord.
Like a canopy of fire.
Like a fortress of light.
Like a shield that sings back to the storm.

We are not exposed.
We are not abandoned.
We are not forgotten.

We are the ones who love Your name—
And Your name is our banner, our breath, our battle cry.

SO WE DECLARE:
We take refuge in You.
We rejoice in You.
We sing in the shadow of Your wings.

Let the enemy rage.
Let the winds howl.
Let the darkness press.

We rise with joy.
We roar with gladness.
We fight with praise.

We are the sheltered.
We are the singing.
We are the ones who rejoice beneath the shield of His name.

But let all who take refuge in you be glad; let them ever sing for joy. Spread your protection over them, that those who love your name may rejoice in you. — Psalm 5:11(NIV)

BATTLE CRY
of the Arising Defender

This is a **Battle Cry** to declare God's unwavering response to oppression. This cry is for those who stand in covenant with the broken, who war on behalf of the voiceless, and who believe that divine protection is not passive…it is thunderous.

We do not ignore the groan. We do not turn from the cry. We rise because He rises.
Because the poor are plundered,
Because the needy groan,
Because injustice dares to speak—
The Lord arises.

He does not delay.
He does not hesitate.
He does not ask permission.

He rises with fire in His eyes,
With justice in His breath,
With protection in His hand.

He defends the broken.
He shields the vulnerable.
He silences the voice of the accuser.

We stand with the groaning.
We fight for the plundered.
We war with the Defender of the weak.

We do not tolerate oppression.
We do not excuse cruelty.
We do not forget the forgotten.

We are protectors of the poor.
We are advocates for the afflicted.
We are warriors of mercy and justice.

We rise because He rises.
We speak because He speaks.
We protect because He protects.

Let the enemy tremble.
Let the oppressor fall.
Let the heavens hear our cry:

The Lord has arisen—
And we will not be broken.

"Because the poor are plundered and the needy groan, I will now arise," says the LORD. "I will protect them from those who malign them." — Psalm 12:5 (NIV)

BATTLE CRY
of the Answering God

This is a **Battle Cry** created to speak directly into moments of distress, invoking the covenant name of the God of Jacob as both shield and answer.

We do not stand alone. We do not cry into silence. The name of the God of Jacob surrounds us.
When distress rises like a flood,
When the enemy presses in,
When the night refuses to break—
We call on the Name.

Not just any name—
But the Name that wrestled with Jacob,
That renamed him Israel,
That built a nation from a groan.

May the Lord answer you.
Not with delay, but with fire.
Not with silence, but with strength.
Not with distance, but with deliverance.

May the Name of the God of Jacob protect you.
Like a fortress that cannot fall.
Like wings that cover the broken.
Like thunder that drives back darkness.

We declare:
We are not forsaken.
We are not forgotten.
We are not fragile.

We are shielded by covenant.
We are answered by mercy.
We are protected by the Name.

So let distress come—
It will not consume us.
Let the enemy roar—
He will not prevail.

The Lord answers.
The Name protects.
We rise in confidence.

May the LORD answer you when you are in distress; may the name of the God of Jacob protect you. — Psalm 20:1 (NIV)

BATTLE CRY
of Unshakable Deliverance

This is a **Battle Cry** that speaks into seasons of hardship and spiritual warfare. This cry is for those who walk through fire and still proclaim the faithfulness of God.

We do not fear the trouble. We do not bow to the storm. We rise
because He delivers.
The righteous may be surrounded,
Pressed on every side,
Struck by sorrow, shadowed by trial—
But they are not forsaken.

Trouble may roar,
But it does not reign.
Pain may linger,
But it does not define.

The Lord delivers.
Not from some—
From all.

From the pit and the snare,
From the lie and the lash,
From the grief that grips the soul.

WE DECLARE:
We are not fragile.
We are not forgotten.
We are not finished.

We are righteous by covenant.
We are upheld by mercy.
We are delivered by fire.

So let the troubles come—
They will not consume us.
Let the trials rage—
They will not break us.

We rise in the name of Deliverance.
We stand in the strength of Redemption.
We shout in the face of adversity:

The Lord delivers—
And we are still standing.

The righteous person may have many troubles, but the
LORD delivers him from them all. — Psalm 34:19 (NIV)

BATTLE CRY
of the Ever-Present Refuge

This is a **Battle Cry** to declare divine strength, unwavering protection, and the unshakable presence of God in every storm.

We do not run in fear. We run into fire—because our refuge is not a place, it is a Person.

God is our refuge.
Not a hiding place, but a fortress.
Not a shelter from battle, but a stronghold within it.
We are not exposed.
We are not abandoned.
We are surrounded by the strength of the Almighty.

God is our strength.
When our arms grow weary, He lifts them.
When our hearts grow faint, He fills them.
When our courage wanes, He roars through us.

We do not fight alone.
We do not stand alone.
We do not fall alone.

He is ever-present.
Not distant. Not delayed.
He is here—in the chaos, in the silence, in the storm.
He is help that does not hesitate.
He is power that does not fade.

SO WE DECLARE:
I will not fear.
I will not faint.
I will not fall.

Trouble may rise,
But we rise higher.
The enemy may press,
But we press deeper into the refuge of God.

We are the covered.
We are the strengthened.
We are the ones who stand—because He stands with us.

Let the earth shake.
Let the waters roar.
Let the darkness rage.

We will not be broken.
We will not be moved.
We will not be silenced.

God is our refuge.
God is our strength.
God is our ever-present help.

And we are still standing.

God is our refuge and strength, an ever-present help in trouble. — Psalm 46:1 (NIV)

BATTLE CRY
of the Unbroken

This is a **Battle Cry** for moments when pressure mounts, confusion swirls, and opposition strikes, yet the spirit remains unshaken.

We are pressed, but we do not break. We are struck, but we do not fall. We are the unshaken—because God is with us.
We are hard pressed on every side—
But we are not crushed.
The weight may come,
But it cannot collapse what God has fortified.

We are perplexed—
But we are not in despair.
Confusion may swirl,
But clarity comes from the One who holds the plan.

We are persecuted—
But we are not abandoned.
The world may turn,
But heaven never does.

We are struck down—
But we are not destroyed.
We may fall to our knees,
But we rise with fire in our bones.

We are the unbroken.
Not because we are strong,
But because He is faithful.
Not because we are fearless,
But because we are filled.

SO WE DECLARE:
We are pressed—but we endure.
We are perplexed—but we trust.
We are persecuted—but we are loved.
We are struck down—but we rise.

God is our strength.
God is our clarity.
God is our defender.
God is our resurrection.

And we will not be destroyed.

Let the pressure come.
Let the confusion rise.
Let the enemy strike.

We remain.
We endure.
We overcome.

We are the unbroken.
We are the called.
We are the kept.

And we will not fall.

We are hard pressed on every side, but not crushed; perplexed, but not in despair; persecuted, but not abandoned; struck down, but not destroyed. — 2 Corinthians 4:8-9 (NIV)

BATTLE CRIES

For
Miracles

Miracles Still March Through the Earth

> This is a **Battle Cry** that will pierce the darkness and release the light and the reigning power of Jesus to overwhelm you with your miracle

We do not serve a silent Savior.
We follow the One whose hand still stretches,
whose name still shakes the heavens,
whose power still pierces the impossible.

Miracles are not memories—they are movements.
Signs are not stories—they are strategies.
Wonders are not whispers—they are war cries of heaven.

"While You stretch out Your hand to heal..."
We declare
— The hand of Jesus has not withdrawn.
— The name of Jesus has not lost its authority.
— The Spirit of Jesus still ignites signs and wonders in our midst.

We rise in this truth
Miracles still happen—because Jesus still reigns.
Healing still flows—because His compassion still burns.
Deliverance still breaks forth—because His name still commands.

So we cry out
Stretch out Your hand again, Lord!
Let signs blaze across the battlefield.
Let wonders thunder through the broken places.
Let the name of Your holy servant Jesus
be lifted high—until every sickness bows,
every chain shatters,
and every heart knows:
Miracles still march through the earth.

While you stretch out your hand to heal, and signs and wonders are performed through the name of your holy servant Jesus. — Acts 4:30 (ESV)

When Miracles Speak, Faith Awakens

This **Battle Cry** roars God's wonders. It Gives us confidence to call forth miracles and believe the impossible is truly possible.

You said it, Jesus—
"Unless you see signs and wonders, you will not believe."
So let the signs blaze.
Let the wonders roar.
Let belief rise like fire in the bones of the doubting.

We do not shrink back from the miraculous.
We do not apologize for power.
We do not dilute the supernatural to comfort unbelief.

We call forth miracles—not for spectacle, but for awakening.
Let blind eyes open and hardened hearts tremble.
Let the name of Jesus be exalted in healing, deliverance, and divine reversal.

We declare ⊢———
— The miraculous is not manipulation—it is mercy.
— Signs are not distractions—they are divine invitations.
— Wonders are not rare—they are the rhythm of a kingdom that cannot be shaken.

So we cry out:
Stretch forth Your hand, O God of glory!
Let signs and wonders pierce the veil of unbelief.
Let the doubters see and fall to their knees.
Let the skeptics be silenced by resurrection power.

We are not ashamed of miracles.
We are carriers of the miraculous.
We are witnesses of the impossible made real—
because Jesus still speaks, still heals, still reigns.

Let belief be born in the blaze of Your wonders.
Let faith rise in the wake of Your signs.
Let the world know:
Miracles still speak—and Jesus is Lord.

So Jesus said to him, "Unless you see signs and wonders you will not believe." — John 4:48 (ESV)

Miracles Happen—Right Here, Right Now

This is a bold, declarative **Battle Cry** that radiates the power of Jesus' name and the undeniable reality of miracles.

We don't whisper it.
We don't water it down.
We shout it from the rooftops:
Miracles happen!

Not someday.
Not somewhere else.
Here. Now. In His name. **Jesus!**

"And His name—by faith in His name—has made this man strong..."
We declare
— The name of Jesus is not a relic—*it is a weapon.*
— Faith in Jesus is not passive—*it is power unleashed.*
— Healing is not hidden—*it is happening in full view.*

Perfect health. Public restoration. Undeniable strength.
This is what happens when Jesus steps in.
This is what erupts when faith collides with His name.

We cry out:
Let every weakness meet His strength.
Let every sickness bow to His authority.

Let every onlooker become a witness to wonder.

We are not waiting for miracles.
We are walking in them.
We are not begging for signs.
We are bearing them.
We are not hoping for healing.
We are heralds of it.

So we shout it again
Miracles happen—because Jesus lives.
Miracles happen—because faith still moves mountains.
Miracles happen—because His name still breaks every chain.

Let the world see.
Let the doubters watch.
Let the glory of God be undeniable.
Miracles happen. And we are living proof.

And his name—by faith in his name—has made this man strong whom you see and know, and the faith that is through Jesus has given the man this perfect health in the presence of you all. — Acts 3:16 (ESV)

BATTLE CRY

Mountains Move When Miracles Speak

This is a fierce, faith-fueled **Battle Cry** that roars with the authority and the unstoppable power of mustard-seed faith.

We do not cower in the face of impossibility.
We do not tremble before towering obstacles.
We speak with the fire of heaven in our lungs—
Because miracles answer to faith.

"If you have faith like a grain of mustard seed..."
Then let the mountains hear us now:
MOVE.
SHIFT.
CRUMBLE.
BE CAST INTO THE SEA.

We declare
— Little faith is still lethal when it's rooted in Jesus.
— Small seeds birth seismic shifts.
— Nothing is impossible when heaven backs our voice.

We are not waiting for signs.
We are the sign.
We are not begging for wonders.
We are the wonder.
We are not asking mountains to move.
We are commanding them.

So rise up, warriors of mustard-seed faith!
Speak to the sickness.
Speak to the lack.
Speak to the fear.
Speak to the generational strongholds.

**Miracles are not rare—they are our rhythm.
Mountains are not permanent—they are our proving
ground.
Faith is not fragile—it is fierce.**

We shout it with fire
**Miracles happen when faith speaks.
Mountains move when Jesus reigns.
Nothing is impossible—because we believe.**

He said to them, "Because of your little faith. For truly, I say
to you, if you have faith like a grain of mustard seed, you will
say to this mountain, 'Move from here to there,' and it will
move, and nothing will be impossible for you."
— Matthew 17:20 (ESV)

The Miracle Is Guaranteed

> This is a **Battle Cry** for those who believe the impossible is possible through Jesus Christ our King. It is a covenant promise from the foundations of the creation.

This is not wishful thinking.
This is not fragile hope.
This is a **guarantee from the mouth of Jesus Himself**.

"Truly, truly, I say to you..."
When the Son of God repeats Himself,
He's sealing a promise in fire.

Whoever believes—
Not the elite. Not the perfect.
Whoever.
That means **us**.

We declare—
— The works He did, we will do.
— The miracles He performed, we will carry forward.
— The power He walked in, we now walk in—because
He went to the Father and sent His Spirit to dwell in us.

Greater works.
Not lesser echoes.
Not watered-down wonders.
Greater.
Because the miracle is not just possible—**it's promised.**

So we rise:
To heal the sick.
To cast out darkness.
To speak life into the dead places.
To move in boldness, knowing heaven backs every step.

We cry out
Let the doubters watch.
Let the skeptics scoff.
Let the mountains tremble.
The miracle is guaranteed—because Jesus said so.

We are not waiting for signs.
We are the generation of greater works.
We are the living proof that the Word still walks,
still heals,
still reigns.

The miracle is guaranteed. And we are the ones who believe.

Truly, truly, I say to you, whoever believes in me will also do the works that I do; and greater works than these will he do, because I am going to the Father. — John 14:12 (ESV)

By These Hands, Miracles Break Forth

> This is a **Battle Cry** for those who believe when heaven touches earth, the impossible becomes routine.

We do not serve a passive God.
We serve the One who moves through His people—
who works wonders through willing hands.

"And God was doing extraordinary miracles by the hands of Paul."
Not ordinary. Not expected.
Extraordinary.
Because when heaven touches earth, the impossible becomes routine.

We declare.
— These hands are not empty—they are vessels of power.
— These lives are not common—they are conduits of glory.
— These moments are not random—they are marked by divine intention.

Miracles are not reserved for the past.
They are erupting now—through those who believe,
who stretch out their hands,
who walk in obedience,
who carry the fire of the Spirit.
So we rise:

To lay hands on the sick and see them recover.
To speak life into dead places and watch them rise.
To confront darkness and see it flee.

We cry out:
Let God do extraordinary miracles through us!
Let signs and wonders blaze through our obedience.
Let the name of Jesus be magnified in every healing,
every breakthrough,
every act of faith.

This is our war cry
Miracles are not rare.
They are rising.
They are roaring.
And they are moving through our hands.

And God was doing extraordinary miracles by the hands of
Paul. — Acts 19:11 (ESV)

The God Who Works Wonders

> This is a **Battle Cry** to stir faith, awaken awe, and declare the unstoppable power of God among the nations:

You are the God who works wonders—
not in secret, not in silence—
but in full view of the nations.
Your might is not hidden.
It is known. It is roaring. It is rising.

We declare
You split seas and shake mountains.
You send fire from heaven and breath into dry bones.
You heal, restore, redeem, and resurrect.
You are not a distant deity.
You are the **God of now**—
the God who moves among His people with signs and
power.

We cry out
Let wonders break forth in our generation!
Let miracles mark our families, our cities, our legacy.
Let the awe of God return to the earth.

We will not settle for natural outcomes.
We are people of the impossible.
We are carriers of divine might.
We are witnesses to wonders.
So we rise—

with faith that defies fear,
with praise that pierces darkness,
with hands ready to release heaven.

You are the God who works wonders.
And we are the people who will proclaim them.

You are the God who works wonders; you have made known your might among the peoples. — Psalm 77:14 (ESV)

Rise—Jesus Christ Heals You

This is a **Battle Cry** to stir faith, activate healing, and proclaim the authority of Jesus with immediacy and power.

We do not beg for healing.
We **declare** it.
We do not wait for signs.
We **release** them.

"Aeneas, Jesus Christ heals you; rise and make your bed."
One sentence.
One name.
One moment—and everything changed.

We proclaim
Jesus Christ heals—now, not later.
The bed of affliction becomes the platform of testimony.
The name of Jesus breaks paralysis, silence, and delay.

We rise with this cry
— Every sickness must bow.
— Every chain must break.
— Every delay must dissolve.

We speak to bodies: **Rise.**
We speak to minds: **Be restored.**
We speak to spirits: **Walk in wholeness.**
This is not suggestion.

This is **spiritual command.**
By the authority of Jesus Christ,
we speak healing,
we expect movement,
we prepare for miracles.

Immediately, he rose.
So we declare:
Let the immediate power of Jesus flood this generation.
Let healing be swift, visible, undeniable.
Let the name of Jesus be exalted in every restoration.

We are not passive.
We are not powerless.
We are the voice that echoes heaven's decree:
Jesus Christ heals you—rise!

And Peter said to him, "Aeneas, Jesus Christ heals you; rise and make your bed." And immediately he rose.
— Acts 9:34 (ESV)

Signs Follow the Sent

> This is a **Battle Cry** to ignite boldness, affirm divine partnership, and declare that signs still follow those who preach with power.

We are not alone.
We are not powerless.
We are sent—and the Lord works with us.

"And they went out and preached everywhere,
while the Lord worked with them
and confirmed the message by accompanying signs."

This is our cry:
We preach with fire.
We move with authority.
We expect signs to follow.

We declare ⸺

— The message is not empty—it is charged with heaven's power.
— The mission is not ours alone—the Lord walks beside us.
— The signs are not optional—they are the seal of divine partnership.

Let the blind see.
Let the lame leap.
Let the oppressed go free.
Let the gospel be confirmed with miracles, wonders, and glory.
We are not spectators.

We are messengers of the miraculous.
We carry a word that heaven refuses to leave unverified.

So we go—
into homes, into cities, into nations—
with boldness in our mouths
and miracles at our heels.

Signs follow the sent.
And we are the ones who go and preach in the name of Jesus.

And they went out and preached everywhere, while the Lord worked with them and confirmed the message by accompanying signs. — Mark 16:20 (ESV)

Grace Speaks, Power Follows

This is a miracle-saturated Battle Cry to honor perseverance, bold proclamation, and the divine partnership that releases signs and wonders through human hands.

We do not retreat.
We remain.
We do not whisper.
We speak boldly—for the Lord who confirms His word with fire.

"So they remained for a long time, speaking boldly for the Lord, who bore witness to the word of his grace, granting signs and wonders to be done by their hands."

This is our cry:
Grace is not passive—it is powerful.
The word is not empty—it is explosive.
Our hands are not ordinary—they are instruments of wonder.

We declare
— We will not be silenced by delay, resistance, or fear.
— We will speak boldly, even when the ground shakes.
— We will remain until heaven breaks through.

Let signs erupt from our endurance.
Let wonders flow from our obedience.

Let the Lord bear witness to every word we release.

We are not waiting for miracles.
We are **walking in them.**
We are not asking for signs.
We are **marked by them.**

So we rise—
with grace in our mouths,
with fire in our hands,
with boldness in our bones.

The Lord works with us.
He confirms His word.
He grants signs and wonders.
And we will not stop speaking.
In Jesus' name!

So they remained for a long time, speaking boldly for the Lord, who bore witness to the word of his grace, granting signs and wonders to be done by their hands.
— Acts 14:3 (ESV)

About the Author

Theda Vaughan is a devoted wife, mother, proud grandmother, and visionary entrepreneur rooted in Greenville, South Carolina.

Theda burns with a passion to see God's people rise in the fullness of their authority in Christ Jesus. She carries a fierce conviction: **We live in a fallen world that wages war against the children of God and passivity is not an option.**

Her cry is for the family of God to awaken, to recognize the power of speaking God's Word aloud, and to wield it like a weapon of victory. She believes that when believers declare truth with their mouths, faith is fortified, the enemy is bound, and mountains begin to move. Theda refuses to let the body of Christ roll over and accept defeat. Jesus overcame Satan with spoken words and so must we. It's time to fight back, speak up, and walk in the authority that's already been won.

More from
Theda Vaughan

theda@warriorprayerbooks.com

**Warrior Prayers Conversations with God
Oraciones de Guerrero Conversaciones con Dios**

Both available NOW on Amazon and other online booksellers!

THANK YOU for buying this book of Battle Cries!

If you find this book helpful in your faith walk, please consider leaving a review on the listing.
This small gesture helps in a big way sharing the Word of God!

www.ingramcontent.com/pod-product-compliance
Lightning Source LLC
Chambersburg PA
CBHW032225050726
47591CB00001B/266